RETURN
LIFE AFTER MORAL INJURY

MARCUS FARRIS, MS

CONTENTS

ACKNOWLEDGMENTS

I N THE STORIES AND myths of ancient cultures, the hero was the person who could descend into the spirit world, the world of the dead, and come out on the other side alive—with a gift of life for his or her community. Real life stories of those who have made this descent have a million different versions, and the gifts of life take many different forms.

The book you are now holding is largely the product of one of these stories, that of Magnus Johnson. His story involved an accumulated 36 months of combat service, most of those in a Special Forces capacity, followed by a return home which was comprised of no small amount of turmoil, grief, and, ultimately, growth.

His story intersected with mine as I was going through my own dark night of the soul in January 2020 in my first days working for his non-profit, Mission 22. Now well-equipped with the life-giving "elixir" from his years of recovery, entrepreneurship, and post-traumatic growth, he imparted many of these lessons on to me—challenging me to grow and cultivate my grief gift in my own way.

This work would not exist without his enduring support as well as that of the Mission 22 team.

DISCLAIMER

THIS IS MISSION 22'S book for helping its readers understand, on a deeper level, how to heal and thrive after experiencing moral injury.

While there are portions of this book that speak to the medical model of care as it relates to mental health struggles following trauma, no part of this book is meant as a guide to replace medical advice.

The first several chapters discuss at length the dynamics of storytelling, the importance of archetypes, and the hero's journey, while the latter half of the book is much more focused on the practical application of these ideas.

The reader should understand that any details provided here with regard to lifestyle practices, such as movement, diet, or use of mental health-related medications, is purely informational and is not to be taken en lieu of formal medical guidance.

Such changes, if desired, should conducted be under the supervision of qualified medical personnel.

THE RAVEN

In storytelling traditions worldwide, this bird has come to represent an agent sent from the divine world to feed, provide wisdom, and facilitate messages from one world to another. A symbol is an entity where two worlds overlap. The symbol of the raven overlaps ancient wisdom with the contemporary struggles of mankind, providing a kind of restorative omen or reminder to discouraged prophets or warriors that their Higher Power has not forgotten their hardship.

INTRODUCTION

For Alabamians, August holds a sacred significance on the calendar. The beckoning autumn transition comes with it the most exciting season of the year where scores are settled on the gridiron between some of the most dominant college football programs in the country.

On August 1st, 2013, my Auburn Tigers had not even made it into the preseason coaches poll. Many of our star athletes from the storied, national-championship-winning 2010 season had moved on. We just signed our new head coach, Gus Malzhan. Our team has historically been the underdog, so it was probably not the dumbest bet to suppose we didn't have much of a chance at making much noise among the top 25.

But by the time the muscadines were harvested and the crepe myrtles had shed their flashes of purples and reds in preparation for cooler November temperatures, things were changing for the Tigers.

On November 16th, 2013, we had climbed our way up to number seven with just a single loss against LSU and were matched up against a number 25 ranked Georgia ahead of the "Deep South's Oldest Rivalry."

After three hours of offensive blows, we were one point short of Georgia's 38. With one final chance, QB Nick Marshall, set up in shotgun formation, had 36 seconds on the clock, and lobbed a "home run" ball, as the announcers said, straight into double coverage. The ball appears to head right into the hands of one of the safeties. The defender stretches his arms out to intercept the ball and seal the game.

But one miscalculation changed everything.

At that exact moment, his own teammate ran into his back, causing the ball to ricochet off his shoulder pads. For a small eternity, the South held its breath.

The football sailed for another five yards right into the waiting and unbelieving hands of receiver Ricardo Louis, who ran straight into the endzone to finish the game in Auburn's favor. To say that Jordan-Hare stadium erupted into an unparalleled state of biblical ecstasy is to say nearly nothing. What was later dubbed "The Prayer in Jordan-Hare" got its own Wikipedia page.

Just two weeks later, during the most bitter rivalry game in the sport, the team would once again outdo itself.

By the time the Iron Bowl rolled around, fans were starting to refer to the 2013 squad as "The Team of Destiny." The players were beginning to believe that they could take it all the way to the championships this year. A rare thing for the program. Would that all change after facing a number one ranked Alabama team?

After yet another three grueling hours on the field, it was our opponent's turn to snap the ball for the last play of regulation. We were tied at 28 and they sent their special teams on the field for a desperate attempt at a 57-yard field goal. Their kicking unit had been struggling all night. The game clock read "0:01." If they made this field goal, they'd have their ticket to the SEC Championship game and a chance at a third straight appearance at the BCS national title.

The Auburn defensive coordinator had cornerback Chris Davis post up in the endzone to receive the kick as if it were a punt. I learned that day that it's actually within the rules to return a field goal kick in that way, but when would that scenario ever actually play out?

Bama snapped the ball and the kick was away, headed right between the uprights…before falling short into Davis' hands. The next twenty seconds would live in infamy as perhaps the most played highlight reel in all of college football history as Davis carried the ball from one endzone clear to the other for an unheard of 109-yard return, sending Auburn to the SEC Championship game instead of Bama. The apoplectic radio announcers abandoned all decorum and composure as their brains could not believe what their eyes were seeing. "OH MY GOD! AUBURN WINS! THEY'RE NOT GONNA KEEP THEM OFF THE FIELD TONIGHT!"

The legendary "Kick Six" also has its own Wikipedia page.

The Tigers went on to defeat Missouri at the conference title. The final game of the season would be held in Pasadena, CA at the Rose Bowl where they faced an undefeated Florida Seminole team for the top position in the country.

A curious thing happened among the student section at Auburn games that year. As our season began to defy expectations, fans started carrying huge orange and blue signs emblazoned with a single word: BELIEVE. This was a throwback to Auburn's creed, written in 1943 during the war, which has the line "I believe" included in all eight stanzas.

We fought hard at the Rose Bowl that year and suffered a heartbreaking loss in the second half. The other team always gets a vote which is what makes the sport so compelling. Still, no one would have picked us for a championship game that season, let alone the overall title. Malzhan became one of only three coaches in SEC history to lead his team to a title victory during his first season as head coach. The previous one was in 1947. The Prayer in Jordan-Hare and the Kick Six highlighted one of the biggest, most unexpected turnarounds for any NCAA football team. Just a year earlier, we finished the season with a dismal 3-9 record.

In 2013, we believed.

* * *

Before diving into the rest of this book, it's important to check our mindset ahead of exploring these weighty topics. Beliefs—the things we tell ourselves repeatedly—surrounding a life change make all the difference in making such a change real. If we encounter new information that could potentially influence a major transformation in our lives, it becomes mere trivia if that information does not lead to action. The new actions which characterize true growth after moral injury are the real-world displays of underlying beliefs about how we are to move forward.

Many systems and "isms" in this world have centered around various modes of teaching someone how to make their lives better. Do this. Think that. Feel this way. It's true that some of them do provide psychological relief to those who are hurting. For example, cognitive behavioral therapy centers around the evaluation of someone's thought life and the interrupting of dysfunctional patterns in favor of more beneficial ones. But what I would offer here is that systems of thinking, feeling, and doing must first revolve around the principle of becoming. If you are not the type of person who would be willing to engage in the process of disrupting old thought patterns in the first place, then the whole enterprise is at stake. What do we believe about that process of becoming? What do we believe about how much growth potential we have?

My two favorite productions of Gordon Ramsay's are *MasterChef* and *Kitchen Nightmares*. In the latter, the host visits failing restaurants to see what he can do to help. For many of the episodes, the pattern is almost always the same. The owner, typically a stubborn old man stuck in his ways, has his way of doing things and is not willing to allow other opinions into his perspective. Over the course of the episode, the audience is treated to confrontations only Ramsay could master, with a volley of insults, told-you-so's, and whatever else the master chef has cooked up for that episode. Eventually, Ramsay and his team do a complete remodel of the restaurant and furnish a clear path ahead for the owner to go down. So, the question is, will the restaurant owner choose that new path?

Not always.

You can Google some of the stories of where the restaurant ended up after having been given every chance in the world to succeed and some of them don't. How could they have squandered such a gift? The reason is because the owner did not see him or herself as someone who could change. They were not willing to *sacrifice* the status quo for something far, far better. The exterior changed, but the heart posture remained the same. The nightmare of the kitchen was simply an extension of the owner's heart that was unable to adopt a better dream for a far more successful enterprise.

We can access all the information in the world with a few taps and swipes on our phone, but if that information does not lead to us taking responsibility for making changes, nothing will happen. If nothing changes, nothing changes.

What do we fundamentally believe about ourselves? Do we believe we can really be agents of change—authors of our own stories? Do we believe it's possible to be free from the clutches of attachment to lesser desires, to substances, bad relationships, perpetual adolescence?

We may have seen radical life change happen in others—witnessed the before and after photos that are so popular on social streams—but do we actually believe it can happen in our own lives? Making that jump requires *faith* in the process, because making one change for one day is merely a single brick in the wall of the cathedrals we hope to build. And our immediate awareness of the present can cause us to have a difficult time seeing the bigger picture. But part of being human means we can conceive of the future. It means that we can understand the utility of making sacrifices in the present for the sake of something that has not even happened yet.

Real faith in the process is not a blind endeavor, either. Participating in faith means participating in the possibility of a future for you and those you care about. Faith is an action we take based on the trust we place in something we believe to be trustworthy. Operating on faith allows us to realize more of our potential and not be slaves to our past.

We treat potential as if it's a real thing. The older you get, the less of it you have. We believe that and behave as if it's real, even if it's not scientific, per se. It's awfully hard to measure in the same way you measure gallons of water in a pool. Potential is a concept only known to the human mind. And in order to flesh out what was once only potential requires a paradigm of operating on faith. Faith that the sacrificial process works. Faith that your drill sergeant does in fact have your best interest in mind. Faith that your life has more potential yet to be realized, no matter what's happened before. And, as I hope to convince you, even more potential if you've experienced something traumatic.

But even with good evidence that the process works for others, it's challenging to fully believe it ourselves unless we *experience* it. And knowing trivia is not the same as an experience. Belief that it's possible is a prerequisite. As Napoleon Hill puts it in *Think and Grow Rich*, "There is a difference between wishing for a thing and being ready to receive it. No one is ready for a thing until he believes he can acquire it." Thus, we have to allow ourselves to be vulnerable to new experiences, inspired by a growth-oriented belief, so that something new can occur in our lives.

Whether you think you can or you can't, you're right.
—Henry Ford

The action of faith follows belief as a glove is moved only when the hand is put into it. Full comprehension and a thorough academic understanding of all the topics on trauma or moral injury is by no means a necessary step. Too often we have this tendency to want to understand things in their entirety before taking the next step, but that's not a good strategy; there's always going to be more to understand, but attaining a complete understanding cannot be the prerequisite for taking action. Where understanding ends as it inevitably will, belief and trust must take over.

Do you believe things can be different for yourself? If so, where in your actions is that belief made real? Our outcomes in life are products of our belief system, and the amount of effort it takes to adopt one belief system over another is the same.

Don't wait to fully understand to take action. If you believe in the right process, that is enough.

Belief is the chassis that our actions and behaviors are built around. It either limits us or makes us limitless. The list below demonstrates several limiting beliefs that might impair our ability to make changes.

- All or Nothing Thinking: I'm either the best or I must be the worst.
- Over Generalizing: "Everything is always bad," or "Nothing ever works for me."
- Negativity Bias: discounting the good while amplifying the bad, placing special emphasis on failures and filtering out the successes.
- Jumping to Conclusions: Assuming we know how things will turn out.
- Catastrophizing: Making mountains out of mole hills, or identifying one small fault and labeling our whole lives with it.
- Overly Emotional Reasoning: Assuming that because we feel a certain way, we must label that with a negative value judgment. "I feel embarrassed, therefore I'm an idiot."
- Frontloading Judgement: Usually characterized by placing "shoulds" and "oughts" onto ourselves or other people.
- Labeling: A form of all or nothing thinking, placing a one word descriptor on ourselves or others and supposing that is the only word needed. "He is just stupid." "I am just a loser." etc.

Limiting beliefs are the downstream effect of old, ossified habits. We think these thoughts automatically about situations without thinking about our thinking.

Think of a limiting belief like the route you take to work. Maybe all this time you've been taking a route that takes much longer than you feel it ought. You know there must be a better way of getting there, but traversing the old, longer route has become so automatic that we are hardly aware that we are doing it.

We draw our mental maps based on beliefs and they become so familiar to us, like the water a fish swims in but is scarcely even aware of, that we easily take them for granted as something that will never change.

I've had a lot of worries in my life, most of which never happened.
—Mark Twain

Why are they there? Who knows. Maybe it was something your parents said or did to you, maybe a girl you asked out to prom at age sixteen rejected you and left a foul imprint of how the opposite sex treats you, maybe you were bullied relentlessly, or maybe there is residual trauma in your DNA left there by an ancestor who never fully dealt with it. While we might never fully understand why left-over beliefs exist, we can choose today to take action of updating these beliefs, thus updating our life.

First, we must become aware of these old belief-based habits in order to do something with them. We'll talk much more about awareness practices in the chapter on meditation, but suffice to say that we cannot hope to change a pattern of thinking if we are unable to articulate what that pattern is.

Old patterns of thinking, to change, must be challenged and confronted. It's the process of the fish becoming aware of the water around him—that thing that we always occupy but don't realize we can do anything about it. There will be a period where two ways of thinking may be at war with one another in the mind, fighting to take up residence. While not an easy thing to deal with, we must continually take action in accordance with the belief system which facilitates our growth in order for it to fully live in the body, especially when another one has already taken up residence.

The process is uncomfortable because it requires killing off an old way of being, and we may not even know what living a healed, fulfilled life feels like at all. The devil you know is better than the one you don't, as the saying goes, and without a vision for something new, our souls tend to wither and cannot see the possibility of spiritual recovery and growth.

But there's another saying, "faith is the evidence of things hoped for." You can read "faith" as *actions* based on your beliefs. If you hope for a transformed life, the bridge between those two places is supported by acting out in faith that change can occur and that you are the type of person worth the effort that will be required.

This begs the question, what is the best belief to have in order to live a meaningful way, especially in light of the tragedy and heartache all of us experience in one form or another? And could one person have the audacity to tell another person what to believe when everyone's experience is unique to them? We all have different experiences, so could it be that a singular belief is appropriate to offer to everyone as a remedy to everyone's experience of heartbreak?

Let's take the widespread success of Alcoholics Anonymous's (AA) 12-step program as an illustration.

One of the criticisms of the 12-step program, first pioneered by Bill Wilson in the 1930's, was its over-emphasis on "the God part" and that those with an agnostic or atheistic background may find this as a stumbling block.

However, consider that since AA's founding, its program has been overwhelmingly effective in allowing its members to find freedom from addiction and has far out performed other interventions. It has succeeded where so many others have failed because of the **belief system** it starts from. AA's members acknowledge that alcohol has power over them, and the only way they can regain that power over alcohol is to allow the power of God into their lives, in whatever way God presents himself to the individual.

When men stop believing in God, they don't believe in nothing. They believe in anything.
—G. K. Chesterton

I once attended a few open AA meetings to get a feel of what the group was really about. One man recounted his early days of recovery and how his sponsor was helping him understand the spiritual aspect of the journey. Now, this AA member was not exactly a regular church goer and had a bad taste in his mouth for the American version of Christianity that he'd experienced. But he knew he needed God. So, what did "spirituality" mean outside a formal religious structure?

"Larry," his sponsor said, "For you, spirituality is returning the shopping cart back to the corral."

The simple act of living in such a way that is mindful of other people, placing someone else's needs above oneself, was enough for Larry. He has since built on that action, but that was the single first step—just return the shopping cart. Do it again the next time, and again the next time. With enough reps, you begin to live your life for other people and one day become a sponsor yourself to someone sharing the struggle of your younger self.

While this book is not a manual for addiction recovery, understanding how beliefs affect outcomes is a really important point to drive home here. Below are the original 12 steps designed for Alcoholics Anonymous, but have since been applied to all sorts of other addiction treatment plans:

1. We admitted we were powerless over alcohol — that our lives had become unmanageable.
2. Came to believe that a Power greater than ourselves could restore us to sanity.
3. Made a decision to turn our will and our lives over to the care of God as we understood Him.
4. Made a searching and fearless moral inventory of ourselves.
5. Admitted to God, to ourselves, and to another human being the exact nature of our wrongs.
6. We're entirely ready to have God remove all these defects of character.
7. Humbly asked Him to remove our shortcomings.
8. Made a list of all persons we had harmed, and became willing to make amends to them all.
9. Made direct amends to such people wherever possible, except when to do so would injure them or others.
10. Continued to take personal inventory and when we were wrong promptly admitted it.
11. Sought through prayer and meditation to improve our conscious contact with God as we understood Him, praying only for knowledge of His will for us and the power to carry that out.

12. Having had a spiritual awakening as the result of these Steps, we tried to carry this message to alcoholics, and to practice these principles in all our affairs.

Alcoholic or not, there's a reason these 12 steps work. And all of us, according to Russell Brand's description below, are addicted or dependent to one thing or another. The difference of living under the tyranny of addiction or past trauma is our beliefs which drive our thinking about our place in the world.

**Addiction is when natural biological imperatives, like the need for food, sex, relaxation or status, become prioritized to the point of destructiveness.
It is exacerbated by a culture that understandably exploits this mechanic as it's a damn good way to sell Mars bars and Toyotas.**
—Russell Brand

It may be the case that we were designed to be dependent on something. After all, there are all sorts of externals our body relies on to keep going. We need good nutrition. We need social groups. Babies will perish even when fed if they lack physical touch. We are dependent creatures. So, the idea isn't to practice having no desires, or to eliminate our drive toward things. The idea is to become dependent on something higher than ourselves that won't let us down the way objects and people in a broken world do.

This is why there is a faith step involved. Our beliefs drive our faith, and what we place our faith in determines what we are dependent on. What we become dependent on determines our path of recovery, resiliency, and antifragility.

ON ASKING FOR HELP

On the battlefield, when is it appropriate to call for a medic and when should the warrior buggar on with the mission and take care of a wound later?

There is a hierarchy of injury, and helpers have a process to sort the wound and treatment based on the level of need and availability of resources. This is called "triage," a sorting process to ensure that resources are appropriately allocated to the need.

In an actual combat situation, it's much more straightforward to triage based on rate of blood loss, immobility, and consciousness—on the physical symptoms of the injury—than it is to triage based on a mental health injury. We use 9-line medevacs in the military to call for help from the medics. The details on the 9-line help the medics to come as prepared as possible to meet the need of the injury.

You don't send in a Black Hawk to evac someone for cracking a tooth because they held their M203 at the wrong angle and the recoil hit them in the face. You also don't just hand ibuprofen to someone who just lost an eye to shrapnel. Still, both scenarios need help administered as the wounds are legitimate. But the particular needs for those wounds must be communicated to the helper in order for the injured party to be assisted in an appropriate manner.

For someone experiencing a mental injury of some sort, there should also be a degree of triage so that the appropriate levels of care are given to the need. "Go see the Counselor" might not be the correct type of help for the situation just as a tourniquet is unnecessary for a stomach ache. But for the helpers or those high in the chain of command, they can be made to feel like they've done something to help because, well, at least they did something. Meanwhile, the type of help given simply does not serve the casualty, and it's a lot less obvious when the wound is of a different variety than those needing stitches or a replacement tooth.

War and life leave mental injuries, and there are a vast amount of resources available—medics, if you will—to meet the need of these injuries. But it's up to the individual to submit their "9-line" in a way that most accurately represents the need. Nine-lines exist for a reason, but we have a harder time sending up the request when the injury is psychological, even if, in the long run, the psychological injury is even more deleterious than a broken bone or laceration—both of which heal on their own with time and a proper healing environment.

Psychological injuries, of course, don't heal merely with the passage of time and the application of time alone does not heal all wounds, that's for sure, especially unseen injuries. Asking for help requires a sacrifice of a type of pride. One type says, "I'm too good for help." The other says, "I'm so good, I should receive all the help." These kinds of thinking have to go in order to make room for the humility that says, "I need some help at the moment so I can pursue a life of healing."

Let's explore the differences.

For some, there is a stigma against asking for help when it comes to a mental injury. Wounds of the psyche are not terribly well understood amongst the general public, and as we've already seen, even experts in the field are punching above their weight class in many ways. Asking for help for an injury of the mind could be an endeavor loaded with pretext. "I don't want to burden anyone else with my problems." "I don't need help because a mental injury isn't that big a deal." "Even if I did ask for help, I would only be judged and given medication. They would just call me crazy." "This pain is mine alone to bear."

While there is a sliver of truth in some of these, it is not the full truth. Medics and helpers exist precisely to help carry the burden of injury. When a good counselor, coach, friend, or other person you might consider a "doc" or "medic" in your context is given the opportunity to lend their aid, it is often not a burden to them, but a blessing. Asking for help from a helper is like asking a bird to sing—they were made for it, and the good ones understand this. (Helpers can definitely be taken advantage of though, which we'll get to shortly). Unseen injuries are often harder to bear than the ones you can see. Some might judge you, but you ought not take advice from or care about the opinion of someone who does not have your best interest at heart.

To allow ourselves to be consumed with the type of thinking that stands as a barrier to submitting a "9-line" is to be consumed with a sense of unhelpful pride. It's okay to take pride in an achievement that produces a benefit to your community, but pride taken too far is missing the mark. Having so much pride that we dismiss the genuine care that others are happy to dispense is a form of thinking that must be sacrificed in order to find real healing.

On the other side of the coin is a sense of entitlement held by the injured—another type of destructive pride.

Seeing oneself as an entitled victim is an unproductive belief system because viewing things through the lens of "other people *owe* me this or that because of what I've been through," keeps the individual trapped in their injury. It's not healing. It's not freedom. It's dependence on other people whom you have no control over to do things on your behalf. It's dependence on a substitute.

This idea leads to a codependent relationship between the one seeking charity and the one giving charity. *In the extreme*, it's a cycle of manipulation by the wounded—guilting others to provide for the poor victim of trauma—and a savior complex developed by the helper, feeling good about being needed and indulging in that sense of self-righteous satisfaction, because at least they're doing something they feel they are good at, perhaps not realizing the trap.

This pattern is disastrous for intimate relationships where either one partner begins to see themselves as the perpetual helper, experiencing an identity crisis when their spouse gets better, or the wounded member sucks dry everything the other has to give with little awareness of when the line of advantage-taking is crossed. Many a divorce have been instigated as a result of the inability to reconcile a new state of affairs post-recovery journey.

There is a never-ending cycle of the victim dipping into the gumball machine of charity (broadly speaking) and a pleasure sensation felt by the helper. But long term, this is not truly freeing for anyone involved. Long term, it is the manifestation of an unwillingness to experience legitimate suffering—a pattern of lasting mental illness perpetuated by a system that stands to gain enormous amounts of social credit and funding based off victims retaining their trauma.

There is a tremendous incentive for the helper in this scenario to keep their victim victimized, and the incentive works both ways. The wounded individual takes advantage of the helper when he or she cannot eventually step into a role of shouldering the burden themselves and moving on with their life *after they have been helped*.

Again, there can be a time for pills, free supplements, therapy pets, and other financial and resource aid. This is *not* a critique against those services as such. But if that is the enduring paradigm—that one's recovery is always dependent on whether or not the VA, a local charity, or family member dispenses another gum-ball—then one stays forever chained to an imperfect machine of trauma care and recovery.

When should we call for a medic? When we recognize we have a legitimate need, a very real injury we need help for—and once that need is met, let the medic move on.

Songs and poetry, and all good art for that matter, express things that we have a hard time expressing through other means, so let's look at two examples that may help with this idea of asking for the right amount of help and taking ownership of our progress.

The song *Timshel*, by Mumford and Sons, grapples with themes of coldness and death, but also of brotherhood, helping relation-ships, and personal responsibility. The title of the song refers to an ancient Hebrew word which essentially means that it is up to the individual to make the choice of how they respond to something they think is unfair or unjust. It might be translated as "thou may-est" as in what God says to Cain right before Cain kills his brother Abel. The point was despite all the things out of Cain's control, the hurt he felt, the sense of inferiority he had, the cards life dealt him, when it came to the most important moral decisions, Cain always had a choice, whether to be resentful and murderous because he thought life wasn't fair, or to carry the burden of responsibility and to live in faith through an apparent encounter with injustice, that is, the rejection of his sacrifice. Cain could choose to kill off the part of him that was bitter, or turn that killing power toward some-one else. We'll look a little more at that story later.

The medic or helper cannot have faith on your behalf that there is a new life waiting for you on the other side of the trauma that we all fear healing from. Fear is a normal response to experiencing the reality that a part of you needs to die off in the form of a sacrifice. For who wants to kill a part of himself?

Your medics are there for you to lean on when your leg is broken, but you must take the steps to allow that leg to heal and walk again.

Next is a profound lesson from the movie *Life of Pi*. In the movie, there is a scene where Pi encounters a very strange island while he is lost at sea. The island provides nourishment during the day, but at night, turns carnivorous. So, while it's good to stay for a moment, that island is not home. That island represents temporary help which may facilitate the choice to live out a new life with humility and proper, healthy attachments to friends and family and the helpers in your life. The other choice is to continue to be eaten from the inside by either a refusal to ask for help or a codependent reliance on a helping system that was never designed to move mountains on your behalf.

Choosing to leave the island is the same as making that sacrifice of pride that is absolutely required to heal from a moral injury.

* * *

As we progress in this book, we will start with a survey of the world of mythology, story telling, and psychology to gain a better understanding of the deeper levels of soul wounds and how to live and grow through them. All the chapters will have actionable takeaways based on the principles discussed. Chapter Seven is the fulcrum chapter of this book which coheres many of the lessons from the first six chapters into practical applications of spiritual healing. The final chapters focus more on the "body" side of the mind-body healing project. While taking actions to help heal your mind and body may seem simple on the surface, it's no simple thing to rebuild a personal philosophy of the world after you've experienced something deeply profane. That's what these pages seek to make accessible.

My hope with part one of this book is to address some of the deeper, more profound demands of the deeply wounded—to look honestly at the darkest parts of this human drama and to address them according to what we believe is a way to understand them anew. I can't claim to have answered every question about the problem of pain, nor can I take credit for coming up with the answers. But out of the collapse and rebuilding of my own faith through the realities of betrayal I have found these principles to be my guide in a world of chaos.

CHAPTER 1

A FRAMEWORK FOR MENTAL DISORDERS

THE FIELD OF MENTAL health as a clinical practice is less than 150 years old. Psychology and the array of psychological disorders as defined by the medical literature are in their infancy. While we've come a long way from some of our more archaic practices concerning the mentally sick, we need to at least recognize that in the 21st century, psychology is by no means at all a hard science as, say, physics is.

The famous Rosenhan Experiment conducted in the late 60's revealed just how tenuous a grasp the medical field had on psychological disorders. In the experiment, a group of about a dozen psychologically healthy "patients" each went to a different asylum located in areas representative of various socioeconomic demographics to see if they could get themselves admitted. Each of them only had one complaint they gave to the psychiatrist: hearing voices. Based on that report alone, the experiment volunteers were diagnosed with either schizophrenia or bipolar disorder. The next phase of the experiment involved the "patients" trying to get out of the hospitals, demonstrating what would otherwise be considered sane behavior. However, they were not permitted to leave until they had undergone the breadth of their treatment and could be considered "in remission."

David Rosenhan, the psychologist behind the experiment, and one of the fake patients, documented his findings in *Science* in 1973 naming his publication "On Being Sane in Insane Places."

Now, it's not as if psychiatry hasn't changed since then, nor is it the case that it is not subject to change in the future. The point to understand here is that it is far from an infallible institution and to turn solely to that field for psychological health would be to dismiss just how much we don't know about treatment of such conditions. I would offer that even today the current paradigm is still woefully insufficient at producing sustainable cures for all its patients. This is an argument that is tacitly made throughout this book. While we will be conducting examinations of post-traumatic stress disorder, the reader may understand that we are using this as an illustration of a bigger point, that psychological well-being and the pursuit thereof is based, in the mainstream, on an insufficient framework.

The thing we now call "PTSD" only appeared in the literature in 1980. It, whatever "it" is, has had 80 different names over the last hundred years—like soldier's heart, shell shock, battle fatigue, combat stress, and so on. Is this condition merely a byproduct of modern styles of combat, unknown to the ancient world?

Whatever this condition is, it is not a recent phenomenon, but something observed by the ancients. In Homer's *Iliad* and *Odyssey* epics, the return home from combat was a 10-year affair fraught with as much adventure and hardship as the journey to battle. Many of the character's struggles—especially that of Achilles and the betrayal he experienced perpetuated by none other than his commanding officer, Agamemnon—are parallels of how we describe PTSD in the 21st century.

The Israelite King Saul as described in 1 Samuel experienced many symptoms of post combat trauma: busts of anger, mood swings, and rage.

So why all the attention on stories from thousands of years ago? Because the older the problem, the older the solution. Healing from trauma is not a new problem.

American culture does not have a transition phase from combat to civilian life like the ancients did. A "purification" of some sort is a prerequisite to enable a warrior to realize him or herself as a warrior who has returned home, as opposed to one who is re-experiencing elements related to war in its various forms, despite the combat being over.

American Service Members have fought in a combat zone within the same 7-day period that they were flown back home to shop for groceries. This is not what the human psyche is meant to do and it's an entirely unreasonable and irresponsible expectation placed on redeploying warriors. Without a transition phase, for most intents and purposes for the warrior, the combat isn't over, even while they're browsing the cereal aisle.

In such a scenario, the mind, without a purification process, is still operating in a mode responsive to an abnormal situation. Hypervigilance, strong recurring memories of threats, and a general distrust of any environment outside the immediate base are all reasonable responses to fighting a war. For selecting produce, such an operating system is less than ideal, but it doesn't make it pathological, necessarily. A soldier is not mentally ill for mistaking a routine errand for a combat patrol if the soldier hasn't performed that ritual of transition.

Maybe why someone displays signs of PTSD in benign environments isn't the question. Maybe the question is more like, how is it that someone once primed for extreme, acute threat deterrence can shift back into a mode of calm and stability?

"Disorder" in PTSD implies that the individual diagnosed is faulty in some way. Now, is there a threshold wherein someone has such a significant amount of psychological distress that one could rightly say that their life is disorder in some sense? Yes, for sure. Is it possible that that individual may need more rigorous clinical help to get stabilized before engaging in a well-rounded health and wellness protocol? Definitely. But can we say that conventional clinical care provides a cure? A lasting remedy? Or, like a cast, do these solutions offer someone the chance to engage in real, deep healing through other means while the hidden wounds are temporarily put to rest?

Below this threshold for disorder, we will refer to the condition as "PTS." "Post-Traumatic Stress *Response*" is another designation that could be more helpful, as the body's response to moral injury (see Chapter Two) shouldn't be surprising. "PTSD" here will be used in reference to the condition as described by clinicians under the current model. Where that threshold lies exactly is tough to put a finger on.

We can't exactly pop the hood on the psyche like that with such precision. The American Psychological Association has hundreds of psychometric tools that are used clinically to aid in elucidating where someone might be on a spectrum of "mental illness." But this is a tricky business because there is not a clear gauge where past a certain point, we can definitively say someone has such and such a condition. It helps in filing for insurance, but these tests are only one data point among many that could be used.

How are we to understand this concept if we cannot measure or perceive it in the same way as a tangible item I could hold? When the clinicians are measuring the progress of one's recovery, it is very often measured using questions about symptoms characterizing hypervigilance, flashbacks, chronic negative emotionality, and degrees of experiential avoidance. The "sickness" as conceived by the diagnosticians can be described in its entirety by a checklist of observable symptoms. The problem with this approach is that a plethora of different symptom presentations from patient to patient could still be classified as the same thing.

Indeed, using a psychometric test to diagnose PTSD per the diagnostic manual, a psychiatrist could identify one of 636,120 different combinations of symptoms and symptom frequencies which would qualify. We just don't know where exactly these thresholds lie and how to describe "it" in as clear and accurate a way as we could the difference between 59 miles per hour and 60.

And is it even the case that we can have a total cure from trauma, or is it something we carry with us forever? Perhaps we can use trauma as something to push against in order to grow from. Maybe we can use the raw material of lead to transmute that pain to gold, to borrow from an ancient Alchemical idea. Of this idea, 20th century psychologist Carl Jung said, "The greatest and most important problems of life are all in a certain sense insoluble... They can never be solved, but only outgrown."

To grow out of this breakdown, the purification journey is necessary because war, or the moral equivalent of war, involves doing battle with the filth of the human heart, with the profane nature of the world.

Today, definitions for mental disorders have been created in order to provide a templated path to healing. While reasonable in theory, in practice, the best our current mental health systems tend to do for the individual is to numb the pain through a pill and brief psychiatric visits to adjust medication. It is a substitute for the sacred purification journey needed after trauma.

The comic strip *Cyanide and Happiness* once published a bit about a patient going in to see a doctor for mental health treatment. "I'm sad," he says. The doctor to him: "Here, take these pills," and he complies. "Are you happy now?" the doctor asks. "I don't care," says the patient. "Good enough!" the physician declares.

This isn't to dismiss psychiatry altogether, of course. Again, there are circumstances where medication can be a first step to recovery, especially in cases of some severe mood disorders. However, as is the case with much of modern medicine as it relates to its treatment of chronic diseases (think: heart disease, diabetes, and cognitive decline), the aim has been to remove the pain now, rather than to prevent or remedy the pain later. The addition of insulin via injection for the type 2 diabetic is a case in point: more insulin solves the here-and-now issue of high blood sugar, but is doing nothing (and even potentially making worse) the underlying issue of metabolic dysfunction and insulin resistance.

Here's one way to look at our approach to treatment from an ecological perspective. In Ancient Rome, in order to feed the blood-lust of the coliseum crowds, the empire began ravaging the local lion population. This allowed the lion's food, goats, to proliferate. The ecosystem became out of balance, and with the vast numbers of goats in the area, some towns were experiencing problems with soil erosion—because the goats' favorite food happened to be the vegetation which held the hillsides in place. Thus, the solution to the erosion in that part of the environment was to allow the predators to roam free. However, our medical model tends to only focus on the erosion itself, so to speak, and gives very little attention to the fact that the predators are missing. There is far less money to be made by allowing the lions to return, allowing the ecology to heal naturally to its balanced state.

Psychotropic medications aimed at taking away the pain now are over prescribed to a frightening degree. As of 2021, at least 65 million Americans have been prescribed at least one psychiatric drug. Five years before that, the number was 40 million. The pervasive, but false, notion that mental illness is a product of a chemical imbalance in the brain has led to misleading advertising and gross over-diagnosis of mental disorders by primary care physicians, not to mention the lack of emphasis on un-diagnosing someone once normal day-to-day functioning is no longer significantly impaired.

In 2022, a review published in the journal *Molecular Psychiatry* concluded that there exists no clear link between serotonin levels and depressive symptoms, despite the fact that about 90% of the public believes the opposite. One of the authors of this study, Joanna Moncrieff, told *The Guardian*, "Our view is that patients should not be told that depression is caused by low serotonin or by a chemical imbalance, and they should not be led to believe that antidepressants work by targeting these unproven abnormalities."

Yet, this chemical imbalance idea has pervaded the mental health culture, by and large absolving the patient of responsibility for taking action to resolve their own problems. This can also be entirely disagentic for the person with the ailment; they no longer sense that they have control over this malaise and instead are now dependent on medications. Recovering from psychological distress has largely been outsourced to interests that are, let's say, not altogether in line with one's own version of well-being.

To drive the point home, consider as well that when a prescription is dosed out in an ostensible effort to cure an imbalance of chemicals, they never tell you what level that ought to be, nor do they take a baseline measure which describes how much the patient currently has and what deficit must be made up. And in any event, even if the clinician did have this capability, would not the problem be one of a biochemical illness, not a psychological one?

To add insult to injury, one of the side effects of taking psychiatric medications can be suicidal ideation. The FDA issued a public health advisory in 2004 with regard to 10 different so-called antidepressant agents:

> *Although no conclusion has been reached regarding the causal relationship between antidepressant treatment and increased suicidality, health care providers should carefully monitor antidepressant-treated patients for worsening of depression or emergence of suicidality, especially at the beginning of treatment and after any change in dose.*

Riddle me that.

Those overseeing these prescriptions rarely, if ever, conduct a full assessment of one's lifestyle as it's related to connectedness with other humans, nutritional factors, physical strength, immune status, sun exposure, vitamin D levels, a subjective sense of self-worth as it relates to achieving meaningful goals, or an analysis of environmental exposure to include unnatural electromagnetic frequencies, micro plastics, and carcinogenic glyphosate, among other factors. What if we were to cover those bases first before ever considering the "erosion control" measure of more prescriptions?[1]

---

1   There is a growing body of clinicians and researchers who are investigating alternative roots of mental health challenges, including Dr. Christopher Palmer, author of *Brain Energy*. His contention is that most mental health issues surrounding OCD, PTSD, and even schizophrenia can be explained largely through diet and metabolism (how well the body can use food energy). Some clinicians just find themselves in a system which simply provides little time or incentive to conduct their practice in such a way to thoroughly examine all these factors.

What if someone seeking help for depression, anxiety, or PTSD was "prescribed" a lifestyle where every day, they ate only whole, natural foods, had a regular fitness routine which included both resistance and cardiovascular exercise, cultivated a community which built close relationships with at least four close friends, followed good sleep hygiene, stopped watching the news, cut alcohol consumption down to two or fewer drinks per week, engaged with nature for hours at a time on a weekly basis, practiced a hobby, and found meaningful work? How necessary would the medical model be if someone followed the basics of living well as a human?

A BETTER CONCEPT OF MENTAL DISORDERS

After the last century and a half of examining what it means to be "mentally ill" or disordered, it would seem we still have a lot of work to do, especially as it relates to the dominant paradigm of treatment. Could it be the case that our First Principles of what it means to be human, the principles which our theories of treatment emerge from, are off? How would we go about separating the wheat from the chaff of all that has come before? I would offer here that first of all, we should examine how the ancients went about the problem, reverse engineer the principles to see how they apply to modern life, and, finally, apply what we've learned in the information age.

So far, I have only expressly mentioned two general categories of mental illness: PTSD and depression.[2] I mention the former as studying its patterns can be very illuminating in understanding trauma and moral injury. I mention the latter because depression in the psychiatric world is a bit like a headache is in the allopathic

---

2 There is another category of mental illness which is concerned with physical impairments of the brain, i.e. neurocognitive disorders, which have their root in physical brain structure abnormalities. This section is not a commentary on those.

world: it's a condition which, in the majority of cases, is there along for the ride, and likely not a sole indicator of the underlying issue.

Since this book is primarily concerned with the patterns of moral injury—again, much more on this idea in the next chapter—much less focus will be given to diagnostic categories. Instead, we are exploring a much deeper underlying pattern that can better illuminate First Principles from which to start. This pattern in my estimation is best exemplified in a warrior returning home from combat, but one need not be a member of this class, let's say, to extract the principles.

To begin this examination, let's look at what the Hebrew Bible said about the transition from a warzone back into the home.

> *Then Eleazar the priest said to the soldiers who had gone into battle, "This is what is required by the law that the Lord gave Moses: Gold, silver, bronze, iron, tin, lead and anything else that can withstand fire must be put through the fire, and then it will be clean. But it must also be purified with the water of cleansing. And whatever cannot withstand fire must be put through that water. On the seventh day wash your clothes and you will be clean. Then you may come into the camp."*
>
> *—Numbers 31:21-24, NIV*

In this instruction to the Israelite soldiers, there are three important components: purification by fire, purification by water, and the passage of a cycle of time. Many a motivational speaker has alluded to the analogy of the refining process, how that which is exposed to heat (that is, trials) and survives is that which is most strong. In metallurgy, this is the annealing process whereby a piece of steel is superheated to the point where the molecules shift their construction and, in the subsequent cooling process, rearrange to produce a much stronger product than before.

So why the association with "purifying?" In the ancient Hebrew conception, mankind is stained with what they call "sin." In Genesis, in Yahweh's warning to Cain, he describes sin as a predatory creature crouching at his doorstep, desirous to have its way with him. It's an entity that can tear us to pieces if we do not learn to subdue it. The Hebrews took sin very seriously, and combat was, and is, a method humans have used to deal with the sins of others. (Of course, no belligerent thinks they're ever the bad guy, and all nations and armies are mixed bags of good and bad, but that's another discussion).

Their solution was to pass that which was stained with the filth of combat—the process to defeat sin—through a fire which burns away dross (the impurities found in precious metals). The problem of humanity is that a lot of what we are is made of dross that needs to pass through a fire to burn away impurities. What, then, does it mean to pass through a trial? It means to voluntarily take on the suffering of becoming a new person, and much of this suffering leaves traumatic scars.

The conceptualization of sin and trial dovetails well with Carl Jung's definition of mental illness. He says, "The foundation of all mental illness is the unwillingness to experience legitimate suffering," sometimes translated, "Neurosis is always a substitute for legitimate suffering."

How about the water part? Well, when something is cleansed of impurity, something else needs to take up the empty space which does not contain that impurity. The filth of combat must be replaced with the purity of clean water. Water here can represent the dialogue needed to process through and renew after an episode of experiencing trauma. It represents knowledge of the *Logos*, or the true speech of God. The water represents something sacred coming in to take the place of the profane.

Finally, the seven day cycle for the Hebrews represents a complete cycle of time for the process to have its effect. It doesn't necessarily translate to needing just a literal seven calendar days to renew oneself after trauma; the point is that it requires a full season of transition before one is fully returned back home.

From these principles, we could say, then, that "mental disorder" is really an incomplete process of refinement. Our struggle to fully realize this completion can manifest in various degrees of "maladaptive" emotional and behavioral patterns. These patterns of affectivity (emotionality) and behavior can always be linked to an outcome the person wants to see occur. We might say that these patterns are maladaptive when we attempt to short-circuit the process of achieving long-term goals, substituting instead negative operating systems to acquire what we think we need.

Animals don't seem to have this problem. Their immediate behaviors are nested in the ultimate, long-term goal of survival. My Australian Shepherd is not concerned that he has variety in his meals, nor is he interested in savoring each bite, which is why I have to buy him a special bowl that forces him to eat slowly, lest he vomit from his rapid inhalation of food. His operating system is based solely on the proximate—the immediate question of how do I stay alive in this moment? However, humans have the cognitive power to relate to the future and to their personal vulnerabilities. Developing a personal operating system, or philosophy, capable of contending with this self-knowledge, is the process of refining ourselves and adapting properly to the story this world presents to us.

How might this play out? If a child grew up in a home where she never knew what to expect from a caregiver, perhaps developing a disorganized attachment style along the way, she might learn that in order to take care of herself, she needs to hide her feelings, steal from others, and lie. She might learn that the only way to meet her emotional needs is to develop attachments to others which are characterized by vacillations between clinginess and avoidance. The story she's adopted is that people mostly likely reject her, and therefore, her behavior must match this story.

We might not blame the child for behaving this way once we begin to understand the conditions of the home she grew up in. But at some point, this child—all of us—must come to terms with the nature of the "dross" inside of us and be willing to engage in a process of burning off the garbage, replacing it with something new, and having faith in a process that could take several time cycles to realize. Failing to do this can lead to self-hatred as we continue to behave in a manner that is incongruent with our stated values, a manner that is instead in accord with the perceived survival state of the child.

THE TROUBLE WITH KNOWING OURSELVES

The process of refinement and purification might be described as a process of coming to know ourselves better. Step four of the 12-step program is to take an honest look at how we're doing, a clear moral inventory of our lives. This process takes courage because when we closely attend to what is inside, we notice a monster staring back. But without this hero's journey of introspection, we act in such a way as to project out onto others the dross that is within us. It's often the case that the thing that most disturbs us about others' behavior is the very behavior we can't stand to see within ourselves.

In the Genesis story, there was a very special tree which opened the eyes of those who ate from its branches. Consuming this forbidden fruit allowed the humans to regard for the first time their nakedness, their vulnerability. For the first time, they were able to truly know themselves and other people, and the first response was to run and hide. The discovery of this vulnerability now made it possible to hurt our fellow man in the most devastating fashion. Because once you know what it's like to be human, you know what it means to feel pain. You know how to make someone else suffer.

Once the toothpaste is out of the tube, there's no putting it back in. Once we realize that we will one day die and that the nature of living is not what we thought, we can't undo that knowledge. We now need a more ultimate objective that we're participating in. This leaves us with a choice. Do we suffer from the cycle of acute pain, numbness, and denial of our death days, or do we suffer from taking on the personal responsibility for shouldering the burden of living fully in light of life's trauma?

The trouble of knowing ourselves is partly why we can be afraid of stepping into a marriage covenant, for example. The reason is because we're afraid that if we truly open up about who we are, our partner will run full speed in the opposite direction. But that's precisely why the marriage is a covenant, so that they don't have that choice. We can never get to learn to sort our own wheat from our own chaff without our souls sounding through with one another. If we don't reveal who we are to anyone, we also cannot reveal it to ourselves. If we cannot reveal it to our own self, how can we know how we should treat ourselves? If we don't know our deeper nature, how can we ever nurture it properly? We could say, then, that allowing ourselves to get to know one another more deeply is in one sense the most selfish thing we can do, since ultimately, it enables us to fill our fulfillment void with the stuff that truly satisfies.

How does all this tie in with mental disorders? I offered before that such conditions might be seen as products of an incomplete refinement and incomplete return home. We all reach a point when we realize that we've crossed the boundary line of the Shire—the

"Ordinary World"—into a land of wraiths and orcs. This realization can crush us if we do not understand what this journey looks like. When we pretend we are still in the Shire even though we are not, when we haven't gone through a refining process, we find that our behavior and emotions are out of alignment—disordered—with what there is to contend with outside the garden.

Hearing and seeing other people's stories also allows us to hear our own story, because they all follow a type of pattern, and it's best when we can see that we need not be stuck in ours, that there is a journey home.

A disordered way of living is a way of living which does not know its story, or the story it has bought into isn't aligned with the truth. An ordered way of living is fully experiencing the tragedy and sufferings of life such that the possibility of turning it into a comedy may indeed present itself.

A WORLD OF MOSTLY GRAY

Legitimate suffering is allowing oneself to sacrifice an old way of being—which views things through a tidier, more black and white lens. The new way of being accounts for the more nuanced kaleidoscopic view that is more representative of our complex world. Every human is a mixed bag of good and bad. We find this truth when one comes face to face with the realities not just of death, but of malevolence. An encounter with malevolence is a bit like that first bite of the forbidden fruit. That bite leaves you with the understanding that there are entities in the world which would exploit vulnerabilities only to satisfy their own ends, and that such entities can first of all be known by looking in.

To use another example from *Life of Pi*—which is heavily set on analogy to the Garden of Eden—the young boy, Pi, explores the tiger cage and gets a little too close to the creature, realizing its power and what sort of damage it's capable of. Ultimately, what we end up learning in the movie is that that predatory creature lives inside Pi. That's the true trauma of the story, not the shipwreck.

Our encounter with an external malevolent force brings us face to face with the reality that that force also lives in us. "Battle not with monsters," Neitzsche said, "lest ye become a monster, and if you gaze into the abyss, the abyss gazes also into you." When we project the monstrous aspect of us onto other things without staring into the abyss, that's when we ourselves become the thing we hated. That's the theme surrounding Luke Skywalker's encounter with his face behind Darth Vaders' mask in the cave.

To avoid becoming the thing we hate, we must gaze into the abyss long enough in order to see the light. To know yourself is to know what sort of bad and good you are capable of. We cannot learn about our potential for good without first learning the bad, as a mountain peak must have a valley to form its shape. It's not enough to strive for returning to a domesticated state, where the peak of our "good" may be summed in an open candy dish. Becoming tame is not the same as becoming dangerously positive.

Tame is like a placated rabbit, capable of docility and of keeping clovers from reaching too great a height, but not much more. A war horse on the other hand bears the image of what we are aiming at. In Jesus' most famous sermon, he states, "Blessed are the meek, for they will inherit the earth." This is no rabbit-like meekness. The Greek word translated "meek" is actually *praus*, which means "disciplined strength." War horses were described using this word in the ancient world. This war horse has a much deeper understanding of what it means to reconcile the realities of evil in human hearts and the potential for much greater good to come from that space.

We all come to a place where sorting things into neat and tidy boxes of good and bad is no longer a tenable option, where we have to put aside our "rabbit-nature." That place where categories are broken is a puncture wound to the soul, a trauma that goes deep and never quite heals right. This is the moral injury. To move forward, we all have a choice to either allow that view to be burned away and refined, or to choose the substitute of legitimate suffering. This substitute is the perpetual refusal of the call to adventure. But, if you remember from Luke's story, the refusal, the indulgence in that substitute, is part of the whole thing. We all refuse to answer that call at first, but that, in our fallen state, is part of the deal.

* * *

To contend with the evil in this world, within our own hearts, we must find something to live for to offset this tragedy. Our best strategy is to find meaning through taking on personal responsibility for the refining process to allow us to reach our personal "apotheosis," the full realization of what it means to be a hero. This means accepting that we will never have complete answers to the deepest questions of life, but that meaning can be found, nonetheless. It will just require legitimate suffering, passing through fire, washing with water, and repetitions. We come to know we are participating in this journey when we understand more fully what T. S. Eliot wrote: "We shall not cease from exploration, and the end of all our exploring will be to arrive where we started and know the place for the first time."

The payoff for experiencing legitimate suffering is that we return home with a new relationship with ourselves and with a remedy for others.

CHAPTER 2

THE WANDERING WARRIOR

WHILE THIS BOOK IS for anyone who resonates with this pattern of moral injury, as with PTSD, we will examine the pattern, or myth, of the hero's journey *primarily* through the lens of the life of the warrior. The fall from innocence and meaning for the soldier on the front lines tells a pinnacle tale of loss, love, and redemption and will be used at several junctions in our discussion together.

As we examine the usefulness of myths and archetypes in this chapter, I will be using the definitions as described by Jungian Psychology. A myth is simply one expression of an underlying form of a repeating human story. In a commentary on Jungian mythology, author Steven F. Walker writes:

That myths can be considered as narrative elaborations of archetypal images (the conscious representations of the unconscious instincts) makes sense, once one accepts the proposition that archetypes were originally "situations," that they are imprinted patterns of behavior left behind by untold

ages of human evolution. Seen from this perspective, myths
are culturally elaborated "representations of situations."
They enable us to re-experience consciously the unconscious
instinctual process of the psyche.

The underlying archetype is like an unseen character template of an aspect of human life. The Jungian would propose that each person acts out an underlying myth, paired with their own idiosyncrasies and that of their culture, and that it's important to know what one's myth is, because perhaps we are enacting a tragedy when we would prefer to be acting out something else. Knowing our myth also helps us in not feeling so alone in our story.

Do the archetypes exist in a sort of objective way in some unseen realm? Are they true? For now, let us say they are true insofar as they are advantageous to helping us reconnect with a bigger thing, placing our moral injuries into a common pattern that can give us ideas as to how to complete the story.

Carl Jung elaborated on hundreds of different archetypal images and how they manifest in a panoply of myths across the centuries. One of the primary aims of understanding archetypes is to be able to describe a core human story to better understand what we are here for. For Jung, this core story describes the archetype of The Self. The Self is a kind of overarching story which has a near endless number of ways to be expressed in overlapping symbols. "The Self operates as the unconscious inner core of an individual's being, as the ultimate principle of harmony and unity," writes Walker. Thus, The Self is sort of composed of a tapestry of sub-story patterns. Some examples of these would be The Wise Old Man (e.g. Obi-Wan Kenobi) , The Divine Child (e.g. Harry Potter), and The Wanderer (more on that later). Here, though, we are focusing on the situation of the warrior, or hero, and examining how that story progresses as a way to shed light on how the reader can do the same.

Joseph Campbell was also a huge influence on how we come to understand the hero's journey in the modern era, how real-life situations can embody that journey, and his conception of that story pattern will also be leaned on.

To sum, archetypes are timeless human situations, the unseen underlying form of a character or motif in myth. Archetypal images are those situations that have been fleshed out with tangible detail.[3] There are an infinite number of ways to put these situations on display, but they all follow a kind of script. Myths are stories which house various archetypal images interacting with one another and addressing timeless human dilemmas. The hero's journey, especially as articulated by Campbell, is the meta-pattern that heroes and warriors of many varieties can see themselves in. The hero's journey —which can be illustrated by the image of a warrior—is the most real representation of the human Self. The hero is that person who embodies courageous self-sacrifice, who voluntarily confronts that which is most scary to them, and out of that, provides something life-giving to everyone else.

Specifically, the warrior archetype is a special type of hero. What sets a warrior apart for the overarching hero's journey that everyone takes part in, in one form or another? Warriors specifically are able and willing to engage in combat. In order to take up this task, a warrior has a heightened sense of the fragility of life and there-fore does not allow himself to fall into complacency. Rather than being callous and uncaring for life as a simplistic reading of combat might suggest, a warrior holds in esteem perhaps more than just

---

3   The reader need not concern themselves too much with the distinction between the use of "Archetype" and "Archetypal Image" here, though the Jungian in his exploration would insist on doing so. Understanding the gist of the significance of a shared cultural story is the main point.

about anyone in society the value of life. A warrior is highly disciplined and knows how to wield the tools of aggression responsibly in life's defense. Warriors have a very strong sense of purpose and understand when to fight, what to fight for, and when and how to prevent fights in the first place. Though they can appear cold on the outside, they have a deep love for those they protect. This coldness and detachment from emotion can be necessary when making decisive decisions as the battlefield requires. Finally, and this is what can be most unsettling to a civilian population who do not understand this dynamic, the warrior is a creative destroyer.

The apotheosis of the warrior is a member of society who understands how to break things down for the sake of creating something new: freedom from an oppressor, *de oppresso liber*. In order for a warrior to live out his fullness, he must put his shadow side under control such that these warrior traits do not turn him into his dark side.

There was a time in history when the warrior class in a culture was a highly honored and revered station. The path of a warrior was well-worn and respected by the culture, and culture provided a sort of buffer for the shadow side of their warrior class, aiding him in tempering and channeling his aggression toward ultimately productive ends. There was a real sense of honor for what it meant to embody the ideals of training oneself to be able to fight for the love of those around them in an ultimately self-sacrificial manner. And there was a deep understanding that with the power and willingness to destroy and fight, such as a warrior has, he needed help to aim that properly.

What does it benefit a culture to pedestalize a group of its members as warriors? Traditionally, it beckoned forth the best out of a society's young men, who might otherwise use their aggression toward lesser ends. The military became a positive outlet for male aggression. It introduced a higher call toward a disciplined life which properly ordered the monster inside into a controlled monster which can protect the society for the inevitability of the next tribe over to encroach on their livelihoods. *The Epic of Gilgamesh* paints just a story wherein the main protagonist was once not much different from a wild beast, before becoming a civilized beast, enabling him to act out the proper role of a warrior hero.

Practicing to become a warrior provided a way to build mastery in difficult crafts. It was a clear path toward virtuous living. And that's all outside the actual combat itself. The culture surrounding the warrior regarded their protector class almost as infants to be protected at all costs; the word "infantry" has its roots in Latin, meaning simply, "a youth." The image is that only the most holy, set apart, pure, and honorable of the society would engage in the act of protective violence.

If all this sounds antithetical to our conception of what military service means today, there's a reason for that.

Something happened around the turn of the century. The enterprise of human conflict went from what was considered an honorable method to settle irreconcilable differences to something altogether profane. Meeting a fellow man in hand-to-hand combat to the death was considered, for most of human history, the proper—even sacred—method to protect one's home and contend with the realities of evil. Now, thinking about war as something sacred might sound barbaric to the 21st century reader. This despite the fact that many highly profitable movies depict exactly this dynamic.

War was no longer a proving ground but a killing field, and the playing out of the archetype of the warrior, at its rock bottom, post-Vietnam, sank to degeneracy. Masculinity itself, associated now with the profane, shadow side of aggression, began to be seen as toxic and unnecessary. In part, the feminist movement was a response to the warriors not living up to what they once were: protectors and providers. But was that the warrior's fault themselves or a broader cultural phenomena? Is anyone or anything in particular to blame, here?

There's this weird schizophrenic response to warriors in our culture today. On the one hand, we'd prefer to have nothing to do with the realities of bloody combat, and sit comfortably in our modern luxuries, labeling the creative destroyers as "toxic." On the other, we feed off digital depictions of this combat all the time. It's like the warrior part of the cultural psyche has been exiled, and the only manner in which we allow it back in is by way of spectacle instead of participation.

War—contrary to the refrain at the opening and closing scenes of the popular video game franchise, *Fallout*—does change. What it meant to be a warrior did as well. The internal conflict of the warrior coming to terms with his capability of destruction certainly repeats, but the introduction of the Gatling Gun, among other technological innovations, provided the option to divorce the warriors from genuine combat—an option Western society opted for. When a platoon-sized enemy unit can be vaporized with the careful manipulation of a glorified video game controller, war has most certainly fundamentally changed.

The loss of genuine combat—especially of culture's relationship to what war means—came with it the loss of what it means to be a warrior. Was technology itself to blame? Perhaps not. Consider that the rates of severe psychological distress characteristic of cases we label PTSD was scarcely suffered among the ranks of the Viet Cong. Why? Johnathan Shey—who first coined the term "moral injury"—says it's because the culture into which those soldiers returned had a better sense of the process of purification, refinement, and the story of homecoming.

Meanwhile, American Vietnam Veterans, tragically, experienced a different story upon their return, a perverse story we are still suffering the consequences from. Almost from beginning to end, the Vietnam "Conflict" was a bad story for the American warrior. To many of the southeast Asians, it was a story of home defense and protection of their way of life. The whole culture participated in the warrior's journey. To the GI, it was many things, but genuine combat aligned with the classic warrior archetype it was not.

Many of them came back home and found themselves strangers in a strange land they had once known. They became Wanderers and the American psyche became dis-integrated. An exile needed to return.

The warrior ethos understands that long-suffering sacrifice is required for peace. In our ten year exchange of munitions and lives with the Viet Cong, such an ethos withered in the face of friendly fire and napalm storms. While there always remains a remnant among society who serve in the military who carry this flame of worthy sacrifice, the dissolution of the warrior archetype writ large continues. And it didn't start with Vietnam. If anything, Vietnam was the culmination of what was set in motion around the time the Civil War came to a close.

What happened over the last 150 years of conflict was that the warrior's sacrifice no longer held a holy place among the wider culture. Truly, it died, at least in the American psyche, along with the last of the Samurai.

In the late 19th century, German philosopher Fredrick Nietzsche declared:

God is dead. God remains dead. And we have killed him. How shall we comfort ourselves, the murderers of all murderers? What was holiest and mightiest of all that the world has yet owned has bled to death under our knives: who will wipe this blood off us? What water is there for us to clean ourselves? What festivals of atonement, what sacred games shall we have to invent? Is not the greatness of this deed too great for us? Must we ourselves not become gods simply to appear worthy of it?

Far from a proclamation, this lament foreshadowed what would happen in the West over the coming years. Without the cultural and psychological moorings to the divine, humanity is left to create its own values through the use of his intellect alone. With this unholy, undying devotion to reason, we invented scientism, forgetting that the original aim of science was to understand how man fit it to God's created order. Our cultural anthropology—our collective understanding of what mankind is—forgot our original nature as described in archetypal patterns and we became our own objects of worship. The inevitable consequence is what happened in the original fall of man as described in Genesis. Mankind, without some conception of a transcendent, stable reality, has no story to unify behind, will fracture and dis-integrate.

When we turn from God, it creates exiles of us all.

So too divorced, in the West, was humanity's sacrificial system of acquiring our basic needs: food preparation, social connections, physical health in all its domains could now become outsourced to substitutes, an option our society opted for. What was once a long-suffering type sacrifice to get what we needed, that genuine "combat" dissolved and became a matter of tapping and clicking. When we can satisfy the needs of the ego by pressing a button, we have surely lost our way.

And as with the warriors who fought in the profane, machine gun-defiled Flanders fields, it began to feel as if our sacrifices were in vain. Is this not why we constantly assure the fallen that it is not so? Perhaps warrior cultures of old never had to affirm this because it was so baked into what being a warrior meant. Of course the warrior's sacrifices weren't in vain. It was as plain as the day was long. Apparently, it is not so now.

The loss of this archetype—the "death" of God—was not purely due to the introduction of new technology. Stealing fire always provides humanity with a choice about how to use it. Do we place this fire within the context of a sacred story, or do we do what is wise in our own eyes and invent our own sacred game?

This choice has presented itself to many generations. Even in the early Genesis account, when man "stole fire" in the form of brick technology, they chose to create Babel. It says:

> *They said to each other, "Come, let's make bricks and bake them thoroughly." They used brick instead of stone, and tar for mortar. Then they said, "Come, let us build ourselves a city, with a tower that reaches to the heavens, so that we may make a name for ourselves; otherwise we will be scattered over the face of the whole earth."*
>
> *—Genesis 11: 3-4*

Rather than honoring God with this new idea of bricks, the people chose instead to listen to their egos, to make a name for themselves instead. This choice removed the tangible piece of tech from the story it was a part of. The innovations of war are our modern day equivalent to the bricks. Now that we have them, what do we do with them? Make a name for ourselves, which leads to fracture and disunion, or serve a Higher Power in humility?

What's new about our generation, though, is the visible scale of the consequences of this choice. The West, at some point, chose to divorce the artform of the warrior (among other artforms) from the technology. This was a grievous mistake. The roots of the word "technology," *technê*, referred to an artform. Technology was a type of creative expression based on patterns of beauty, but we've largely papered over the beauty part for the sake of pure utility, pure reason. (Perhaps one reason for Apple's success, for example, is Steve

Job's attention to the art of *technê*). As Robert Persig, American writer and philosopher, puts it:

> *This divorce of art from technology is completely unnatural.*
> *It's just that it's gone on so long you have to be an archeologist*
> *to find out where the two separated. Rotisserie assembly is*
> *actually a long-lost branch of sculpture, so divorced from*
> *its roots by centuries of intellectual wrong turns that just to*
> *associate the two sounds ludicrous.*

Indeed, divorcing the old patterns of honor associated with the warrior's journey to war, and return home, from the new technologies—this is the loss. It had nothing to do with the technology itself, but of a pervasive unwillingness to apply associations between drone strikes and archetypes. And it also had nothing to do with any one individual choice, but a much greater drift from the roots.

Thus, in the 21st century, we are now faced with the task of returning to this pattern, but doing so with a healthy respect for the dynamics of contemporary life. A common instinct among our current service members is that the military provides a means to experience something outside of, and bigger than, themselves. This instinct, too, is rooted in this deeper warrior archetype. It's a narrative overlay which tethers daily actions to a more important thing.

While briefing a mission, the officer in charge might use a terrain map combined with overlays. An overlay is a transparency, like those write-on-wipe-off acetate papers used for old school overhead projectors, that can be placed on top of the detailed terrain map to show the soldiers locations of key elements to the mission. Different overlays highlight different aspects, like rally points, evacuation routes, or avenues of approach. The detailed terrain map by itself provides no direction. The overlays fitted with the terrain map inform the soldier of meaningful details that enhance his likelihood of mission success—it's the final step in making a plan on paper executable in reality.

But when service members experience a crisis-level confrontation with a culture that, on the whole, has removed itself from an ancient narrative context, a moral injury occurs; the psychological overlays hold little meaning anymore.

How we all go about marrying the divide between an ancient life-giving, peacemaking pattern of living and 21st Century substitutes starts with a recollection of who we are, as Symba was admonished to do from his deceased father. First, remember who you are. Re-member who you are to a higher participation.

I think great artists and great engineers are similar, in that they both have a desire to express themselves. In fact some of the best people working on the original Mac were poets and musicians on the side. In the seventies computers became a way for people to express their creativity. Great artists like Leonardo da Vinci and Michelangelo were also great at science. Michelangelo knew a lot about how to quarry stone, not just how to be a sculptor.
—Steve Jobs

When we forget what the process of getting to know ourselves looks like, we forget that what we need is not merely the service of modern convenience, but to serve ourselves by serving others.

This is the deepest meaning of the warrior archetype that all can learn from. It's a story that's even bigger than national militaries themselves. This is what society gains by revivifying the honor due to the youth who voluntarily takes on the struggles of the world: service is joy.

THE ARCHETYPE OF THE WANDERER

Twenty miles outside Philadelphia, in the winter of 1777, following a series of logistical and moral defeats at the hands of the British Army, Washington and his troops were in need of a new approach. The time spent at Valley Forge brought with it severe losses of combat power due to disease and malnourishment, and the prospect of winning a revolution against the 18th century's strongest superpower seemed grim. Despite this, the Continental Army was reinvented with new standards of discipline, structure, and training, thanks in large part to the influences of the likes of the French nobleman Marquis de Lafayette and Prussian military officer Baron von Steuben.

Lafayette, for his part, organized a group of subject matter experts from various European nations, who had a stake in America winning the war, into what he called the "Corps d'Étrangers." Literally translated, this means "foreign bodies."

This historical example provides an archetypal image of one other story pattern we will examine here, that of the wanderer, also known as the foreigner or stranger. The wanderer is the character in the story whose task is to provide something new and refreshing to some culture, person, or system that has otherwise become locked up in its rigid ways or has fallen completely into disorder and randomness.

Many hero story arcs are characterized by a main character who fits the description of the wanderer. This character is usually rejected by his hometown, lives on the fringes of culture, is a master of two or more worlds, commonly has unknown or unusual origins, speaks multiple languages, sees reality differently, never quite has a long-term place to call home, and, most importantly, has a strong sense of purpose, knowing they have something to provide in order to remedy an entity that has otherwise been taken over by too rigid or too chaotic a system. One of the reasons why "outsiders" seem to make for attractive candidates in politics is because they are seen as a person who can bring a much needed update to a government that has become too set in its ways.

Sinric, one of the more odd characters from the TV series *Vikings*, is revealed to be the soul who tells the main protagonist, Ragnar Lothbrok, about the shores of England and gives him a tool to navigate his longboats to them. Sinric doesn't have much of a place to call home and comes and goes throughout the series in order to provide timely translational assistance between several different cultures. However, the audience never really knows what exactly his origins are.

This expedition ends up bringing a much needed relief to Ragnar's clan and carries the story forward. One of the interesting byproducts of going out on expedition was that they captured a few of the priests after having sacked Lindisfarne, which again brought in another type of foreigner, Athelstan. Ironically, Athelstan and Ragnar end up being foreigners to each other by providing new information about different ways of living, learning each other's language and even partially adopting the other's spiritual point of view. The genius of the storytelling is that between the Saxon and Norse cultures, there are inversions and unexpected story elements that began with the introduction of the stranger into an established culture. The "good" and "bad" guy dynamic is so blended, one often doesn't know whose side to be on.

For a more straightforward example of the outsider archetype, consider a humble ogre. Shrek lives on the fringe of the kingdom and because of his status, is able to ultimately restore balance. Lord Farquaad is this tyrant whose aim is to rid the kingdom of anything foreign. The architecture is all straight and highly categorized. He is obsessive about keeping things clean and orderly. But too much of this prevents the kingdom from ever growing. Enter the foreigner who provides the update. We see that Lord Farquaad, in his quest to keep a tight grip of control is eventually taken out by the chaos dragon—right as he is decaring, "I will have order! I will have protection!"—because he is not willing to allow a foreign body into the rigid kingdom.

The Matrix, *The Book of Eli*, and *The Chronicles of Riddick* all portray a type of wanderer for their main character.

Neo acts as a foreigner because after his own death and rebirth scene near the end of the first movie, he is able to see the source code of the matrix. (The birth-death-rebirth is an archetypal pattern common to a myriad of story types.) Even though Neo had made it so far in his training and was many days past having taken the red pill, his return from the abyss happens when Trinity effectively resurrects him with her love. Neo becomes The One when he allows himself to die off and be reborn. It is then he is able to speak the language of the virtual world and master both Zion and The Matrix.

The Book of Eli shares several characteristics of the wanderer even more explicitly. Eli is able to see differently, ironically, because he is almost completely blind. He reads braille and since his vision is not like everyone else's, he can perceive things beyond normal sight. His wandering involved a very specific destination and his role was to bring order into chaos by delivering the Word of God to humanity's last remaining functioning city. Oddly, the Shrek story, an upside down fairy tale in its own right, is the reverse of this. Shrek brings chaos to too much order where Eli brings order to the chaotic wasteland. The wanderer provides harmony between the two by traversing between cultures, mastering and harmonizing each yet being a full citizen of neither.

Riddick is one of my favorite examples of this archetype. In his story, it's not obvious at first what kind of hero he is. Popular superhero tropes show how their heroes bring balance to two worlds quite explicitly and it often relieves the audience of the challenge of understanding how that works. The "dual-citizenship" between the animal or mechanical and human domains is right there in the names: Batman, Spiderman, Ironman, and so on. For Riddick, though, it's more subtle.

We learn early on that he has polished eyes which allow him to see in the dark. There's a scene later on which has him face to face with this space wolf which was just seen tearing apart others in the penitentiary. Riddick was warned, "Don't look them in the eyes." Yet, because Riddick grew up on Furya and had to adapt to the very unique situations of that world, he had a unique ability to bond with the creature. One of the other inmates stared in disbelief as Riddick had tamed this lethal predator. "It's an animal thing," he says. The tragic part to his story was that his homeworld had been devastated and he was one of only a few Furians left. But of course, in archetypal terms, this makes perfect sense.

There are countless other hero's journey stories which magnify this archetype—Spock the Vulcan, Wolverine, *TRON: Legacy*, Aloy from the *Horizon* video game series, *The Wizard of Oz* and on and on—but one of the most ancient examples comes from the Exodus story. Who better characterized a wanderer than Moses himself? He was born an Israelite, raised an Egyptian and went on to free the Israelites from the Egyptian masters. Egypt was at one point very friendly to the Israelites, but over time, the Pharaohs forgot their original pledge to the Israelite people and became tyrannical. Therefore, it was necessary for this foreigner to tear down what at one point had been a thriving nation. But from Moses' perspective, you could imagine the conflicting allegiances he'd have as an Israelite by birth and an Egyptian by upbringing.

Following Israel's emancipation, his primary role was to lead the nation through the wilderness, literally a wandering leader. That same theme picks up with Jesus of Nazareth later in the Bible. His story, to some degree, stands as an exemplar of all the major archetypes including the wanderer. He wasn't welcome in his home town during his ministry, he was an itinerant preacher for most of his career, he tended to camp in the city's adjacent wilderness (on the fringe), part of his ancestry included members of tribes outside of his line of Judah,[4] and once said, "Foxes have dens and birds have nests, but the Son of Man has no place to lay his head." He didn't have a place to call home. Not in this world, anyway, yet he had an extremely strong sense of purpose that kept him going.

The application of this pattern can be viewed through many levels of analysis. A moral injury in this context might be considered an over-exposure to the fringe of reality, or an over-exposure to another world you didn't think existed or otherwise were not prepared for.

Back to the Riddick story, imagine you were not a Furian and never grew up on a planet with such harsh living conditions (or if you ever had to move to Fairbanks, Alaska, this prospect isn't so hypothetical). If you were suddenly dropped off into this environment, all the sudden you find you are not equipped to master this

---

4   Tribal lineage was a big deal to the Hebrew culture. The fact that Jesus' bloodline was "impure" is symbolically significant as it highlights his role as a sort of beneficial foreigner, a *Corp d'Étranger*, if you will.

territory. A psychological coping mechanism is to bud off a piece of yourself which represents the "you" that had to contend with this new world so that that chaotic part wouldn't sully the part of you that wants to be kept untouched by the foreign body. Perhaps the thing budded off is the shadow you'd prefer not to deal with, like Harry Potter's horcrux.

It's the piece that can survive Furya, but in order to do so, must become a kind of beast—not necessarily a good or bad beast, but a type of monster nonetheless. When we see that beast within us and don't know how to integrate it, we might try to deny its presence. If we stare into the abyss and we find it stares back, it can undo us, but we may overcome it. In *Sleeping Beauty*, the first mistake the parents make is to deny Maleficent an invitation to the palace in hopes of sparing their daughter from ever having to contend with that dragon-witch. But of course that went horribly wrong. Without the integration of the dragon, Sleeping Beauty passes out at the first sign of blood, a pin prick. She's totally incapable of surviving outside her walled palace. Maleficent represents a part of the princess that must be invited to the palace, so to speak.

We'll examine that "part" a bit more later in this chapter, but it can be useful to give it a name for ourselves. Is that part your wanderer? A foreigner? Does it (or he or she as you see fit to think about it) feel like an exile to the rest of your sense of self? How do we bring that internal exile back home? First, understand the pattern.

The injured "you," when it isn't fully integrated into the non-injured "you," will create significant internal conflict until it can be reconciled. Injured "you" (living out the pattern of the wanderer archetype) has a piece of beneficial information that non-injured "you" needs to consume and assimilate. This happens through the archetypal birth-death-rebirth pattern; practically speaking, it's a kind of psychological sacrifice (much more will be said on this later). Neo, Harry, and in his own way, Christ,[5] all realized that pattern in their stories to become fully integrated. When that has happened, you can speak a new language, master two worlds, see things differently and, perhaps at last, provide a psychological space for that hurt to live in peace. The wanderer, when reconciled, creates harmony. This story can be understood at the individual all the way up to the global level, like fractal patterns on a fern.

There is a song by the artist Far Out called *Strangers* which beautifully illustrates what this reconciliation process feels like.

Lately when I look in the mirror
I don't know who I see
These eyes are so much darker
Then they ever used to be
Even when I turn off the lights
And sink into dreams
Everything around me is a lie
Just a memory

I don't know who I am
There's a stranger, just a stranger where I stand
I am just a stranger
I don't know who I am
There's a stranger, just a stranger where I stand
I am just a stranger

---

5   In Revelation 13:8, there seems to be a very close relationship between the sacrifice made on the cross and the genesis of creation. The language hints that the sacrifice happened either before or in conjunction with the creation of the world, which sounds very strange to the linear thinker, but does appear to follow the archetypal hero: he/she must die off for new creation to be made real and for heaven and earth (or mind and body) to be reconciled.

I get lost in crowded rooms
So I don't feel alone
And in every face I still see you
Like I'm dancing with a ghost
Tryna hold myself together
But I feel you in my bones
Every step is one step closer
To never letting go
To never letting go

Once that internal hero's journey has taken place, then the fun work begins. Now you, your unified "you," can provide beneficial information that brings harmony to those in your family and community. On a cultural level, the warrior is that wanderer, but the individual must traverse that path if his or her community is to as well. After playing out the wanderer's story internally, you can then manifest it externally. "As above, so below."

When the warriors come home, society does, too.[6]

WHAT'S IT MATTER?

We've mentioned a bunch of different fictional stories and how they illustrate patterns of historical human endeavors, but now, let's take a closer look at how the abstract domain of archetypes and narratives interacts with the concrete world of tangible things.

Consider the word "matter." There are two meanings that describe two wholly different realms. There is the matter that makes up the material world, and there are things that matter to us. There are descriptions of substances measurable by scientific tools, and there are the rules we play by.

Think of it like the differences between the gameboard with its physical pieces and the set of rules with which you use to play the

---

6   See the practical application of this in Chapter Seven.

game. Or how one deck of cards can have hundreds of meanings depending on the game being played, but it's still the same deck in the material sense.

The rules you use to play the game of life form your worldview and beliefs. These rules are like the water the fish swim in: absolutely necessary for swimming, but easy to take for granted. Though we operate within them every day, they tend to be below the threshold of our awareness. When we have a healthy narrative overlay, it reduces the activation energy needed to complete tasks because we can take for granted that some activities are worth participating in than others.

When I was living alone, it was very easy to dismiss the dirty dishes accumulating in my kitchen. I'd put it off for one or two days a week that were my dish washing days and get it all done in one go, versus cleaning up as I went. I justified this strategy because the effort to get up off the couch for just a few dishes seemed like a lot more effort than doing the dishes in larger batches. The downside was that the kitchen's baseline state included dirty dishes. Once I was living with someone else, I had an updated story. It went from optimizing for just my own liking to optimizing for two people's liking. By shifting this story, the activation energy it took to clean up right after a meal decreased; working for two instead of just one made hard things easier, even though the overall amount of objective work was about the same. This is what an updated narrative overlay can do. When matter matters, it provides worth, direction, and animation to action.

What does it mean to mean something? When something has meaning, it activates a guiding instinct to put awareness on one thing instead of another. On the drive between LA and Sacramento, there is a two-hundred mile stretch of orchards lining I-5. Among the orchards, there is a tree, among millions, with an ant colony, maybe a billion strong, which hosts a whole complex micro-ecosystem that supports life, specifically fruit. The tree is taken care of by machines and farmers who have their own complex stories. But by the time that peach reaches your grocery store, you have filtered out a thousand other stories that could have been told and only let in the one meaningful to you: a piece of ripe fruit for purchase which will contribute to your survival. The last sentence is the meaningful story because it's the one which calls your attention. It carries *weight* for you, where the other ones did not. (And the farmer has his own set of stories which probably don't include you, either.)

To mean something is for something to carry weight which draws attention. Narrative overlays provide the schematic of what carries weight. And there is an element to the narrative which changes over time and an element which remains the same, much like a sense of identity. Moral injury makes the immutable, unchanging part blurry.

Everyone's narrative gets updated over time and we use it like a map that guides behavior. Mythologies and religious moral codes served this role for many cultures, describing the story in which they "occupy" psychologically—the story that tells them how to behave and why. The modern western mind has a tendency to dispense with ancient stories in favor of scientific inquiry, the unnatural split between art and technology if you like. But one cannot be a replacement for the other. Science describes the "gameboard" while story describes the rules by which you play. Science answers: what it's made of and how does it work? Myth answers: what it is for and what does it mean? It's like the difference between a glove and the hand in the glove. These domains are often confused during public discourse on the topics of science and religion, which is too bad because it was from principles drawn from the church that science grew.

Science and scientific endeavor did not grow from the material world. A deck of cards does not present to you how to play a game. Instead, we use a set of rules, or more broadly speaking, a narrative to guide our judgements and decision making through the game of life. Our story is based on our beliefs and our meaning is derived from the story we see ourselves as being a part of. Material in and of itself does not have an intrinsic meaning. It's the story that the material is a part of that bestows meaning, and it's that meaning which humans orient their lives around. We orient around a story which provides a coherent enough rule set—a moral code to live by—such that we can live lives with worth, direction, and animation.

When that story is unable to account for a crisis and fails to allow us to comprehend a situation we encounter, this is called a "moral injury." Moral injury describes an event or series of events that severely damages an individual's moral landscape of the world. It is that close encounter with the abyss, and often associated with malevolence itself. Far more cases of PTSD result from encounters of egregious human behaviors than from natural disasters. Moral injury happens when our old rule book of how we fit into a bigger story is torn to shreds, and it turns out that we may not be the hero we thought we were after all. This could be due to witnessing an action that didn't fit into our old framework, perhaps an action we were unable to prevent or an action we perpetuated ourselves which we thought we were never capable of.

To use our card analogy, it's as if you're playing Five Card Draw and you have a royal flush. Thinking you've won, you go all in, only to discover that your opponent possesses an even better hand that you didn't think was possible because it was outside of your understanding of the rules. You lose everything because you were not playing with a rule set that had been updated with this latest development. This is devastating and calls so much of the hand you were dealt into question. But it's more than a ruleset, it's our sense of our personal destiny. It's our sense of what we've set out to accomplish in our life.

This may also be described as "existential shock." We're shocked when the way we thought things existed turns out not to be fully correct. There is always going to be a hand dealt to us that cannot be accounted for by our current psychological structures. The trick is learning to accommodate more and more of these unknowns in a manner that doesn't take us out all at once. But it doesn't always happen that way.

ON AWE AND DREAD

The wrestling with moral injury we struggle with after existential shock is fundamentally our response to a negative experience of awe.

Awe can be defined as "the emotion experienced during rapid attempts at cognitive accommodation." Experiences of awe can generate a perspective shift away from mundane, day-to-day activities and toward a higher order goal or entity. Awe is the emotion which goes along with a diminished sense of self and the reaction to a more powerful other. It's the emotion that operates along the neural circuitry that gives us goosebumps.

The idea from an evolutionary perspective is that piloerection (hairs standing on end as a result of goosebumps) is a prey's response to a predator. When a prey animal perceives a more powerful other, it makes itself look bigger and more intimidating to increase its chances of survival. It's why cats arch their backs up when they sense danger. In a manner of speaking, the prey is embodying the predatory creature in order to ward it off (more on this in Chapter Four).

Awe in and of itself isn't necessarily positive or negative but depends on context and how one interprets the experience. Seeing the Grand Canyon for the first time is likely a positive experience, while witnessing a JDAM bomb explosion over a fortified enemy position—complete with all manner of ejected debris—is certainly awe-inducing, but perhaps not altogether positive. We'll call the negative side of this experience "dread." One experience might lead to reverence of a higher power, or it could lead to an overwhelming sense of doom.

Experiences of awe and dread are like the forces of gravity surrounding a planet on a nearby starship. Imagine a ship rocketing through outer space and as it gets closer to a large planet with a sufficient pull of gravity, the flight path of the ship changes in accord with the planet's gravitational field, even if there has been no change in the ship's propulsion system. These experiences alter our trajectory of where we thought we were going even though what was propelling us along the way seemed to have worked before the encounter with the planet. The question might be asked, as it has been in some way or another by every culture, how ought we relate to an experience of something, or someone, inconceivably higher than ourselves?

Alluding once again to an ancient way of thinking, Proverbs 9:10 states that it is the fear of the Lord which is the beginning of wisdom. And again, Proverbs 1:29 says that the fool hates knowledge and chooses not to fear the Lord. The Hebrew word "to fear" is the word *yirah*, which is a word that describes both an awesome *and* a terrifying thing. God is an entity which is both dreadful and awesome—and according to the Hebrew authors, the correct response to such an entity is reverence, which in their language is also linked to *yirah*.

In a Hindu story found in the Bhagavad Gita scriptures, the main hero, Arjuna, is called upon to lead an army into a cosmic battle to settle a dispute about which ruling family ought to be in power. On the eve of battle, Arjuna looks over the fields and sees not an endless mass of unidentifiable foot soldiers, but family members, brothers, friends, and colleagues. He breaks down and loses himself at the thought of having to lead so many to their death. Fortunately, the god Vishnu, taking a human form named Krishna, is there to teach Arjuna the nature of the universe. After an unconvincing lecture given to Arjuna, Arjuna asks to see the mysterious makeup of the universe for himself. Krishna obliges and gives Arjuna cosmic eyes to be able to see past the veil. Arjuna is awed by what he finds there as all time and space as he knows it breaks down. He sees that souls are not lost, but rather just change their expression. And in this view, time breaks down and he sees he has already won the battle.

Returning to his formal state, he is now emboldened to lead his family into battle as his new understanding of the universe is so much more vast that the present sufferings are put into an infinite context.

There is a striking parallel between this story and the ancient story of Job. Bruised and broken after being tortured at the hands of The Opposed One (the meaning of the title "The Satan"), Job accuses God of being unjust. For the bulk of the story, Job's friends, representing various perspectives on human reason and wisdom, dialogue with him to help him come to full terms with the loss of his family, health, and all material possessions. At the end of their reasoning, no satisfactory answer is presented. Then Yahweh steps in and challenges the human's conclusions about God's justice system.

God's response? A virtual tour of the universe, posing questions to Job about the origins of mysterious things in the universe. "Where were you when I laid the earth's foundation?" Yahweh asks.

"Who shut up the sea behind doors when it burst forth from the womb, when I made the clouds it's garment and wrapped it in thick darkness?"

Following this tour, Job realizes how small he is in relation to infinity and says, "My ears had heard of you but now my eyes have seen you. Therefore I despise myself and repent in dust and ashes." Then Yahweh gives Job a double portion of inheritance and restores him well beyond his state before the trial.

In both of these stories, the answer to the human cry in the face of dread is an experience of awe. Awe-filled experiences are turning points in stories that take the human heart into, and perhaps out of, the abyss. In light of these stories, we could say that moral injury happens when we encounter a part of God, of "Being," that we cannot fully assimilate.

The God of the Hebrew Bible is presented as a lion *and* a lamb, a single entity comprising an apex predator and a helpless prey. How can one assimilate those concepts on pure reason? The point is that we cannot, which is why a pure experience of the divine, of whatever strikes us as awesome, is the only best response. And we can experience the breadth of awe and dread just by getting to know ourselves and other humans more deeply. Humans are made in God's image, which perhaps means that we each have both a lion and lamb living in us. This is the conflict that if unreconciled, leaves a soul wound unhealed.

In our wrestling with moral injury, we come to see the wisdom in author Frank Herbert's quote from *Dune*: "The mystery of life isn't a problem to solve, but a reality to experience." Put another way, the answer to our sufferings is a game to be embraced, not a game board to be comprehended.

THE SACRED AND THE PROFANE

A sense of dread might be considered that which happens when witnessing or participating in something truly and deeply *profane*, a word which means "to render unholy." Things that are "holy" are things that we consider separate and special when laid against the common things of the world. We all build up internal structures of our own sense of holiness in an effort to reconcile our desire to be good with our very real ability to do evil. A profane life is one in which we do not live with a concrete point of moral orientation, where nothing is set apart, nothing is held in higher esteem than anything else, and everything is common. The idea of "holiness" here means that we adopt a way of living which can objectively rank order degrees of beauty or goodness. The idea is that on the latter worldview, we have a framework wherein we can say that this-or-that behavior, idea, or image is of a higher value than another and thus more worth pursing. But who is to say which things belong where? Moral injury casts doubt on that structure.

In any case, no one person has a perfect ability to distinguish the common from the holy, or the sacred from the profane. And when we encounter something which we consider deeply profane which we have not previously accounted for in our existing worldviews, the temptation is for us to throw up our hands and give up seeking out the holy things. Trauma can leave us feeling as if nothing is sacred. It makes us wonder what in the world matters anymore.

In a profane world, points of meaning seem to come and go without anyone's consent. The stuff that seems to matter appears and vanishes like a vapor. Just when it seems we have a solid philosophy of the world, an event occurs that pulls the rug out from under it. In the book of Ecclesiastes, the author refers to this state of affairs as "meaningless," or *hevel* in Hebrew. Hevel is a word which could describe the very momentary smoke puff from the end of a pipe; you can see it and it appears as though something is there, but you cannot grasp it and it disappears as soon as it appears. The case the author is making is that the world can't be neatly summed up with feel-good proverbs and that there is a lot of *hevel* to contend with—and without a sacred, concrete centering point, it all feels pretty vaporious.

In *The Sacred and the Profane*, Mircea Eliade writes of this meaninglessness,

> *Properly speaking, there is no longer any world, there are only fragments of a shattered universe, an amorphous mass consisting of an infinite number of more or less neutral places in which man moves, governed and driven by the obligations of an existence incorporated into an industrial society.*

From the sociological lens, we might say that our society has become "anomic," or, without norms. The West has largely lost its narrative mooring and a consequence is that we have a much greater difficulty marrying the two definitions of matter discussed before. What characterizes a whole culture which has lost this connection? In Jonathan Height's *The Happiness Hypothesis*, he writes:

> *Anomie is the condition of a society in which there are no clear rules, norms, or standards of value. In an anomic society, people can do as they please; but without any clear standards or respected social institutions to enforce those standards, it is harder for people to find things they want to do. Anomie breeds feelings of rootlessness and anxiety and leads to an increase in amoral and antisocial behavior.*

In the ancient Roman world, the response to their anomic societal tendencies was the development of the philosophy of Stoicism. In our current anomic society, the response has also been, in part, a return to Stoicism. Curious.

The split between art and technology, the loss of sacred things, the rejection of at least some agreed upon standard of norms, and, ultimately, the loss of a unifying narratives and archetypal patterns are all the same thing. Why is technology meaningful? Because there is an artform behind it. Why should we think of some things as being sacred? Because we need to know what is worth pursuing and what isn't. Why do we adhere to cultural norms? Because we must understand that everyone can contribute to everyone else's quality of life.

Why do we need archetypes? Because without a time-honored pattern to follow, we are stuck in the abyss.

Healing from an intense experience of dread and profanity can only be mended with an experience of awe and sacrality. The path through this drama is found in the process of realigning ourselves to a true story, modeled after the archetypes, allowing ourselves to be refined along the way. This is how one's tragedy becomes a comedy, with a rough beginning, but a hopeful ending.

Could it be possible that our modern alternative actually works better? That these patterns which emerged prior to the advent of modern science were fine for the ancients, but are better relegated to the history books and not to 21st century practice? Well, can the current medical model of mental health contend with this present darkness?

Imagine patrolling an Iraqi village when the guy next to you suddenly vaporizes into a mist because he stepped a few meters to the right on a pressure plate while you continued straight. Imagine witnessing the unceremonial loss of a still born child down a dark sewage drain. What do you say to someone recovering from that? What sort of philosophy of the world can account for such things? What amount of cognitive behavioral therapy can deeply mend these wounds?

The problem with an anomic culture is that it does not have a good answer to contend with the reality of malevolence, of evil. Today, its answer is more mental health and prescription medication. If these solutions have, for you, been a deeply healing and lasting cure to your heartache, then don't change a thing. What I would offer is that the depths of the world's profanity are unknown to most people because the old stories have been severed from common life. Scarier still is that those depths are within each of us. We can become morally injured simply by getting to know ourselves better, and most of us don't know what to do when that happens. It seems to me that "more mental health" by itself does not, and was not designed to, fully heal a moral injury.

The return home from the wilderness of moral injury involves acting out a story pattern. We look to how archetypal heroes "come back home" and we embody those character and story components that resonate the most with us. When young children are playing house, they aren't simply imitating the mom or dad, they are extracting out the components of what it means to be a mom or dad, then expressing those embodiments in a kind of game. Or, when a little boy, let's say, is misbehaving, mom or dad might ask the boy something along the lines of, "Is this what a big boy would do? Is this what Spiderman would do?" In essence, they're asking, "Are you acting out the story of a hero or of a child?"

Similarly, grown ups look to archetypal stories to embody in their own lives. It's not that we imitate Captain America by putting on a costume and fighting bad guys (unless you're on your way to Comic Con, maybe); it's that we see that character's bravery and courage in the face of small odds and behave in a brave and courageous manner in our own lives, whatever that may look like. We see that these attributes are preferable to characters which reject their responsibility and act like misbehaving children.

So what is this pattern exactly that we are looking to imitate?

Tony Stark, in the first Iron Man movie, demonstrated this pattern by becoming an even more powerful monster than his captors. He saw what he could have become—just another arms dealer like the terrorists—but reoriented those energies against them. He adopted the monstrous characteristics by lying about what he was doing, deceiving his captors, and even allying himself with a machine which could breathe fire. He embodied the most deadly features of the underworld in order to be reborn into Iron Man. He became part dragon without allowing the darkest depths of the underworld to fully consume him. Pepper Pots, the female side of the story, was the force which kept Tony grounded in the role of a positive, order-bringing force—preventing his inner tendency to descend back into the chaos. This story pattern also contains a foil.

In a narrative, the term "foil" refers to a rival-type character who ultimately serves to highlight the positive attributes of the protagonist. The foil is a part of the story, a feature, not a bug, and ultimately serves to make the hero into who they are. An encounter with dread can become our foil, showing us the terrible things that we and other humans are capable of doing…and capable of overcoming. Malfoy served this role for Harry Potter. Foils are pointers; as dread shows us the consequences of sin, awe shows us what we could become if we hit the mark. The peak of a mountain is defined by its valley. This is the tension we have to live with as we recover. And speaking of Harry, through his whole series, he had to hold the tension of becoming the hero for good while contending with and integrating the shadow, the piece of darkness, within him.

Healing from a trauma is a process of integration and transmutation, of accepting the shadows of our nature and transforming those into a force for good. How can we tell whether we are in that process, when we are hitting that mark?

Archery, as with many sports, involves taking aim at something and striking a target. There's something deeply human about cheering for a sports team aiming at and hitting a target, or witnessing the opposing team shank a field goal leading to your team's victory. We go absolutely wild when a team of 18 to 22-year-olds carry a pigskin down a grass field and cross a painted line. Even testosterone levels respond positively or negatively if your sports team you're watching wins or loses in a game you're emotionally invested in.

What on earth are we up to?

In archery, to miss the target is to "sin." Experiencing a traumatic, dreadful episode can make us realize that our definition of holy, the mark we were aiming at, is so far off from what is actually Holy that we are nearly brought to death by the experience. We have to allow ourselves to burn away all the stuff that is causing us to miss the mark, to go through a refining process. That process is very difficult to put into a step-by-step manual because we are complicated creatures and because when we start talking about morals and souls, we have to speak in narrative terms, not scientific ones. Again, that's why we must lean so heavily on stories and archetypes found within them. The way out of our own abyss journey is to watch and embody another story where a character was experiencing something similar.

To take an example from the sports world again, when a coach is giving cues for an athlete to follow in order to improve her, let's say, clean and jerk performance, the coach cannot get the athlete to experience the texture of someone else's mind in order to see what the procedure is to perfectly execute the movement. The coach must give a series of verbal cues that the athlete then translates into an athletic movement. It is quite the art to be able to use the correct words which result in the athlete embodying a highly nuanced neuromuscular pattern. But good coaches can do it, and adapt to cues that athletes can understand and act out.

In Olympic lifting, learning to brace the core ahead of the lift is extremely important for power transfer. Doing this while explosively launching hundreds of pounds over head involves a ton of refining to get down right. There is no step-by-step series of manual-like instructions that the athlete can follow in order to get it. Rather, the coach might say something like, "Pretend there is a giant coke can in your torso. The bottom of the can is your pelvis and the top of the can is your shoulders. When you brace, do it in such a way that you don't crush the can."

Then the athlete can take that mini story, "Don't crush the can," and embody that cue to perform in a way that hits the mark. Remarkable. Somehow that cue is more helpful than a comprehensive anatomical description of how to fire each and every muscle fiber in the proper series. Stories are our cues to help us hit the mark.

No tree can grow to heaven unless its roots reach down to hell.
—Carl Jung

This process of embodying the right stories teaches us how to render that which was once dreadful into something quite awesome, and it's what the rest of this book is about. In the ancient practice of Alchemy, their "holy grail" was the philosopher's stone, an object which had the ability to turn something common like lead into the most uncommon and precious material in the world in their eyes—gold. While such a literal stone was never found, nor was their thinking in alignment with our notions of modern chemistry, it stands as a metaphor for how trauma can itself be our foil—revealing that out of this experience our lives can turn to gold using the raw materials of a broken soul. The human who has come out of the other side of their descent to the underworld—remade into someone brand new is the most precious creation of all.

This process is not a matter of just learning to think the right way, adjusting our attitudes and feelings about the world, or doing the correct actions that our therapist encourages us to do. It's a matter of willingly putting to death an old mode of being to allow a new creation, an integrated human, to come forth, from whom properly oriented thinking, feeling, and acting will naturally follow.

That matters more than anything.

FUNCTIONS CHECK

1. What fictional stories do you find yourself going back to? Why?
2. In what ways have you experienced profanity? What things, events, or behaviors would you describe as profane?
3. How could you see yourself as a monster?
4. How can your "monstrous" attributes be put in control such that they are in service to others?

CHAPTER 3

DIA LOGOS

I think the most important
question facing humanity is,
"Is the universe a friendly place?"
This is the first and most basic
question all people must answer
for themselves.
—*Albert Einstein*

W E'VE EXAMINED HOW THERE has been a split between art and science, or spirituality and materialism. There has been a widening gap between our culture's unifying narrative with our daily lives. In order to recreate this union, we learn to discover which story we are a part of, then speak it into existence. Many ancient cultures' creation stories involved their using speech to create the world. This, too, is a power we have. The types of things we say, both to ourselves silently and to others out loud, create the world that we live in.

Speech, a dialogue between parts, unifies the bigger story with smaller actions. If we are feeling lost in our struggle to reconcile a moral injury, perhaps we have fallen into a pattern of poor speech. Let's see how the power of speech works in practice.

America was founded based on a declaration of independence—a statement that this group of people is now its own thing. A country was created by words spoken by self-identified individuals. The Declaration was composed of a dialogue and a collection of identities, the body of the document, and the signatures. Those two things together constituted the new boundaries of a country that didn't exist before. Their speech created their world.

Another example. I've worked for a while with a psychological operations unit in the Army and we are taught early on how important messaging in operations is. There's something about the interaction between printed word and the human psyche. This interaction is one good advertisers understand very well. How we behave is heavily influenced by the messages we consume. It's almost like magic…as if "magic words" truly are magic words. The right ones compel behaviors, for good or ill. There is an interaction which occurs between an external leaflet and an internal interpretation which produces a changed behavior. Abra kadabra alakazam and, oh, look, you're buying a product you wouldn't have before seeing the ad. Magic. The advertiser has created or exploited a behavior in its audience using carefully tailored words.

This magic is a dialogue, an interaction that generates a relationship between two or more (dia) parts which contain meaning (logos).

Every invention, every man-made object, at one point only existed as a thought in someone's mind. That thought was translated into a series of words which contained the meaning of the idea. Those words were expressed through speech, writing, and drawing, and once those were better understood, the abstract concept became a concrete object.

A dream produces an idea. Ideas and thoughts turn to words, which turn to a blueprint, which we then turn into something usable and tangible. This is a uniquely human talent.

The world presents us with problems to solve. *Beliefs* about how such a problem ought to be solved generate ideas. The brain is an idea generating machine that often feels out of our direct control. It's not obvious exactly where ideas come from, and one may ask—do we have ideas, or do ideas have us? It seems more likely that the answer is the latter and that our job is to cultivate beliefs that generate productive ideas that lend themselves to the "blueprints" that finally result in a more habitable world.

Our beliefs drive how we perceive the world. Do you believe you need to buy a new Jeep? Now you notice every one that passes you on the road. The belief for a new off-roading vehicle is based on your presumption that such a purchase would enable you to solve a particular problem in your life. When we encounter new problems, we are given the invitation to alter our perspective in order to generate new ideas. It may be that every genuine problem has a solution when one has the correct perspective and is asking the right questions. It's as if by design, like locks and keys, that the fact of a problem is proof of its opposite. So, if you're running up against a problem that seems unsolvable, maybe a perspective update is needed to generate new ideas.

Ideas, when they are first expressed, are not fully formed in words yet. Ever try to explain an idea to a friend and say, "I'm not sure how to say this?" But the idea exists, nonetheless. We talk to ourselves to sort out which ideas ought to die off and which ideas ought to be translated into constructive action in order to solve the problem.

The behaviors that result from adopting new perspectives serve to create a new world—in material objects, in positive or negative relationships, and even in creating a new physical structure of our brain. The things we think, the words we process and linger on in our mind, literally shape the physical structure of our brain and inform our cells how to react to these thoughts.

Be careful of your thoughts, they become your words.

Be careful of your words, they become your actions.

Be careful of your actions, they become your habits.

Be careful of your habits, they become your character.

Be careful of your character, it becomes your destiny.
—Dalai Lama

Beliefs drive perspective. Perspective drives ideas. Ideas drive language. Language creates reality. Negative or positive thinking becomes our brain's shape. The shape of the brain forms the shape of our bodies. The blueprint becomes the structure. The more we think on something, the easier it is to think on it more in the future. Every thought becomes a chemical in the body, a chemical analogue of that thought, helpful or unhelpful. This means, then, that our physical bodies are representations of the story we are telling ourselves.

So, for example, if someone has a learned paradigm of "I'll always be alone," and that thought continues to roll through their mind, the body responds by producing chemical analogues that serve to reward isolatory behavior. The body serves the mind by obeying the thoughts it is fed, translating those thoughts into altered genetic expression and protein production. This mental paradigm of "I'll always be alone" takes up physical residence in the body. If we learn this thought pattern when we are young, we've created a dialogue that creates a host of psychological distresses. Practicing a new dialogue which is in alignment with a better story is how we undo this pattern. This is why a prerequisite to making changes is altering and challenging our existing beliefs like we discussed in the intro.

This is also why it becomes so difficult to break out of old paradigms because you are literally fighting your physiology's programming that it learned from a previous belief system. We create dialogue with our beliefs, and those drive our actions. These dialogues help us perceive a complex world in a way that makes sense to us, but not all dialogues, of course, are equally as life-generating. The dialogue is then embedded within the physical body. You must get in your reps to make the idea of "No, I won't always be alone" (in our example) real in your body, creating a new relationship with yourself.

Sometimes, it can be so difficult to update an obsolete dialogue that all we can do is to simply trust and have faith that taking an action is beneficial. The neural connection in the brain takes almost no activation energy to default to a negative way of thinking. So, when we attempt to change, rather than trying to start in a top-down manner, a bottom-up strategy could be more useful. It can be a lot easier to act against a belief living in the body than a belief living in the mind.

For example, it can be easier to act out being the type of person who doesn't isolate by taking the action of putting oneself in a social setting, before feeling like doing it, versus doing therapy to reroute maladaptive thinking processes which then help to change one's mood before taking action. Feelings follow action. We can change our mind by first moving the body, turning the levers physiologically (within the body) so that the end result will be a shift psychologically. Sometimes, therapy can get this backwards.

In a healing journey, it's not always obvious which dial to try to turn first. Do we target behavior, thinking patterns, or feeling tones? Seems like more often than not, if we wait for the right feeling or the right way of thinking, we'll wait a long time before we change a behavior.

Actions lead feelings.

It's time to workout.

I don't feel like it.

The workout doesn't care. It's time.

Dialogue with the workout, not the feeling. Then you'll feel better.

What I would offer here is that if you have no idea where to begin, just go workout with a group in a manner appropriate for your skill level and limit caloric intake from liquid sources.

But sugar tastes good.

Your results don't care.

But I feel comforted when I eat the sugar.

*The comfort from being physically healthy
lasts a lot longer.*

*But I'm tired and I'm not sure that hard
work is worth it.*

*You can suffer the pain of the work now or
the greater pain of regret later. Choose.*

Just by removing garbage from the diet and getting into a regular exercise pattern you counteract old belief systems that characterize PTS. Don't wait till you feel like it. Don't wait until you have done all the research on which exercise is best. Believe that you are the type of person that is becoming strong and healthy and go.

Sometimes it doesn't have to be complicated if you live by faith.

In some sense, faith is a prerequisite for any action at all. Every decision made is a value judgment that the chosen decision is superior to others you could have made at the time. It's an act from faith that one behavior is preferable over another and that the behavior will result in the outcomes you were after. The future is not guaranteed, and just because something worked last time does not always mean it will work again if you take the exact same action.

Did you have faith that your car would start this morning? Is it always guaranteed to start and function properly? No. There is always the possibility that we might overlook something and that the thing we overlook (like a leaking gasket) can confound what used to be a reliable process. Chaos is mythologically conceived as this monster from the underworld. That's a pretty solid image to describe when things suddenly seem to go wrong out of nowhere. The problem was lurking there all along, just waiting to rear its head.

So, in light of these "chaos monsters," the best option is to live by faith that despite their existence it's still worth taking action to create a better world.

> *If I workout with others,*
> *I might have a panic attack.*

That's true. It's a risk.

> *Okay, so I won't go.*

Staying home is its own risk.

> *Staying home is comfortable.*

Discomfort identifies growth.

How does this work in relationships? We must put faith in our spouses or friends that they will do what they say they'll do when we're not there to monitor them. Overbearingness in relationships from one party or another results from a lack of faith in the other person's future actions. If life were full of actual guarantees, faith and hope would not be required. Faith keeps our eyes oriented toward the higher good, especially in times of chaos.

Maybe that's what Jesus meant when he said, "Your faith has

made you well." (Mathew 9:22). Having faith is taking an action based on something you may not yet fully comprehend but that you comprehend enough to trust the person saying it and to take action. We are made well by aligning our actions with a bigger thing (a person or story, perhaps) that we are in awe of.

So, outside of gym visits and dietary clean up (topics which will have their own chapters), how do we begin tackling an old, outdated belief living in the mind?

In Dr. Jordan B. Peterson's *Beyond Order: 12 More Rules For Life*, rule IX states, "If old memories still upset you, write them down carefully and completely." This concept describes the importance of integrating traumatic experiences into our lives today and updating our psychological map of human behavior.

Moral injury can leave our beliefs fragmented and sometimes our behavior doesn't make sense. We want one thing yet we do the opposite and the next day wonder, "What on earth was I thinking? That wasn't me."

What on earth we were thinking was probably a thought that stemmed not from the belief that we desire but from the belief that lives in our bodies that needs to be relearned.

If we "know better" than to act this way or that, but do it anyway, I would propose that there is a belief within us that reflects a part of us that is not yet integrated—a memory or experience that we have not fully adapted to, learned from, and mined out any useful bits of information to inform future blueprints for creation. We haven't returned home from the moral injury journey, not completely.

Post-traumatic stress, or anything truly traumatic, has the potential to generate flashbacks or intrusive memories. This is the mind's attempt at assimilating a negative experience of awe, of dread. Awe is an experience that current cognitive structures cannot fully take into account. These intrusive memories don't have a home—pain with nowhere to go. They must be integrated into your belief structure before your behaviors can become more coherent with your desired beliefs, and those moments of, "what on earth was I thinking," may begin to diminish. The cognitive dissonance between two beliefs that are seemingly contrary to one another begins to fade away when we choose a courageous path of learning deeply from a past experience.

> ## The unconscious insists, repeats, and practically breaks down the door, to be heard.
> —*Annie Rogers*

Chronic occurrences of these memories change the physical structure of the brain as we already discussed, but the shapes of our brains and bodies are negotiable, as I hope you're beginning to see.

These memories are like a rejected child left outside the house, desperately knocking at the door to be brought in. The pain is never going to go away completely, but we can integrate the pain and allow it to become a part of us in a coherent way, growing our hearts around it.

This is the process of updating a belief system which influences the ideas which create our world. So, what I would propose is that healing from a moral injury allows us to update our world in such a way that we have a *far superior* method by which to problem solve because our belief system has been refined as gold in a furnace. In this light, moral injury provides fertile ground to problem solve in a whole new way.

We can create far better worlds by allowing a moral injury to do its work and to make the necessary sacrifices to heal.

So how do we show some love to that "child" left outside, or the "unconscious" that Annie Rogers is referring to?

Internal Family Systems (IFS) therapy is a methodology which theorizes that parts of the psyche can be "dis-integrated" which causes dysfunction. Older psychoanalytic ideas propose that an individual's psyche is composed of subpersonalities. You can see an unintegrated psyche play out in the behavior of a three-year-old. At one moment, you're talking to the hungry child, then the playful child, then the sleepy child. The "spirits" of hunger, play, and fatigue become dominant personalities at a given moment. The child has little grasp on her ability to inhibit and place boundaries around these subpersonalities because she is not yet integrated.

IFS suggests that when we experience trauma, one of these subpersonalities—or parts—becomes disintegrated. These are the "exiles." Reintegration involves speaking to that part of yourself as if it were another person, to accept the disunion, forgive yourself or others involved in your trauma, and come to terms with the fact that you have the potential both for harm and healing. This is the idea of becoming more aware of both the potential for good and the potential for tragedy we discussed in the last chapter.

It's a process that teaches us to hold the tension between trusting others and putting up our guard. Too much trust leaves us naive and vulnerable. No trust leaves us cynical and unfulfilled.

This reunion can be achieved through professional talk therapy, hand writing letters to your past self or someone else in your life that needs to be forgiven (no one else has to see these letters), an awareness practice like meditation (see Chapter Seven), and by engaging in meaningful conversation with old and new members of your tribe. It is also often the case that there is unfinished business that a relative passed down to you. Maybe your trauma was not originally your trauma, but something a parent, grandparent, or other family member never fully dealt with, but now it's your responsibility nonetheless.

We have looked at this idea of a "previous belief system" that drives our creative forces, and one may ask, where exactly does that come from? Well, in part, it can in fact come from deceased or estranged relatives that passed on the sin, the faulty belief system, on to their offspring. It turns out that by reconciling with family members, we can give them back their unfinished business so that we no longer have to carry it. We can break the cycle of transgenerational trauma by observing what our core language is, ("I'll always be alone, anyway"), asking whether such language actually belongs to someone else in the family, having a dialogue with them of some sort (again, letter writing here can be powerful, even if that person is deceased), and reconciling the hurt by forgiving them and picturing them as wishing you the best in your life.

For a deep dive into that topic with more specific practices, check out the book, *It Didn't Start With You: How Inherited Family Trauma Shapes Who We Are and How to End the Cycle*, by Mark Wolynn.

The most powerful ties are the ones to the people who gave us birth. It hardly seems to matter how many years have passed, how many betrayals there may have been, how much misery in the family: We remain connected, even against our wills.
—*Anthony Brandt*

DIALOGUE NEEDS TRUST

In order for dialogue to do its work, the interlocutors, members of the dialogue, must have a level of trust with one another. If not, then the healing message cannot bridge the gap. If faith makes you well, then trust facilitates the healing message transfer between the one who is faithful and the one in whom faith is placed. When PTS has taken a deep-seated hold on the psyche, trust is a rare commodity. It manifests in the body as an overstimulation of the stress response branch of the nervous system. If the body doesn't think the world around it is trustworthy, it activates the nervous system in a way to prepare for danger and uncertainty. While there are times for this activation, we are not going to live well if we can't learn to trust anything again.

It's no mystery why someone healing from moral injury might have trust issues. Part and parcel of such an injury is that trust somewhere was radically broken.

But rebuilding trust doesn't mean naively trusting everyone all the time. It means that in certain circumstances, you give someone or a group of people the benefit of the doubt. It means extending a small amount of trust to establish a beachhead in what could be a new relationship. Extending trust initially invites the best of the other person to present themselves to you. Rebuilding trust with oneself and others enables one to honestly ask for needs and can free us from thinking we have to perform in a certain way in order to be loved. We begin to see ourselves as someone worth taking care of, regardless of the words people have told us, or indeed, words we tell ourselves.

Trust is an extension of a felt sense of personal security. When we experience what might be the worst form of moral injury, betrayal, (which at some level, every moral injury has a component of) it becomes much more difficult to feel safe at all. In such a situation, we might start by first turning inward. The pain follow-ing a betrayal, in part, is the pain of knowing that we could cause the same pain to someone else. And maybe we did. Thus, we don't even feel safe sitting in a room by ourselves. The two of you don't have a trustworthy dialogue.

I will trust you—I will extend my hand to you—despite the risk of betrayal, because it is possible, through trust, to bring out the best in you, and perhaps in me.
—Dr. Jordan B. Peterson

The immediate aftermath of moral injury may bring with it a coping response, telling us that we're better off *never* trusting anyone. But if that belief persists, we haven't fully learned the les-son. We must come to a harmony between naive confidence and liberal skepticism, landing somewhere near wise discernment. Our boundaries must become like membranes that allow some things in, but still have a shrewd eye on things that should be filtered out.

We have to venture ever so slightly out of our comfort zones, just enough to allow ourselves to be one degree more vulnerable than we were the previous day. Maybe you really don't like being around crowds, but you still need to go to the grocery store. Can you marshal the courage to simply drive to the parking lot during non-peak hours and experience the sensation of being in your car as a handful of people come and go? That's a step forward from iso-lation. That's the process. Reduce down the much larger challenge of blanket distrust of the world to the smallest manageable unit. Maybe after a few repeats of that, you get out of the car and go up to the front door, then go home. After a few tries of that, you make a short list of items, go when the store is least busy, focus on what you came there for, and then leave.

These are the one-degree actions we can take to restore our sense of trust. Maybe it's not crowds for you, but gyms, or relatives, or whatever. But there's always a very small step you can make toward the direction you want to go. No one is expecting anyone to go from living holed up in an apartment due to the overwhelming anxiety of being exposed to crowds to attending a Lakers game overnight.

As you make this progress, finding that balance between engaging in uncomfortable situations and spending time in the comfort zone is negotiable across time. There is a time to engage in uncomfortable settings and a time to regroup in the comfort zone. But spending all your time in isolation, in temporary comfort, is no way to grow.

Everything you want is
on the other side of fear.
—Jack Canfield

While isolation and avoidance satisfy temporarily since they keep us from danger and discomfort, they can quickly become a negative feedback loop. The more we avoid, the less able we are to engage and experience healing and growth. If someone desires to experience post-traumatic growth, embodying the warrior spirit means getting out of that comfort zone and going to that place of fear in measured doses. There is no substitute for taking action in the uncomfortable growth zone.

Is that not exactly what warriors do in training? Measured doses of combat-related stress over time builds courage and resilience in the face of impending uncertainty and danger. The warrior's training at home is the same—it just has different skin on.

On the surface, driving to a grocery store parking lot in order to confront a fear of crowds may not sound anywhere close to being on par with kicking in doors as an infantryman or what have you, but on another level, it is the same principle with a new manifestation. The warrior at home contending with the effects of post-traumatic stress engages in the same process as the warrior downrange. It's just disguised as what the rest of society would consider routine domestic tasks.

The new enemy is this loop of isolation, anxiety, stress, and the challenge of building discernment. Fighting this new enemy will take on a very different appearance than a deployment or field training exercise, but the willingness to engage with what the warrior fears most may be itself the path your archetype is called to take.

For the word of God is alive and active. Sharper than any double-edged sword, it penetrates even to dividing soul and spirit, joints and marrow; it judges the thoughts and attitudes of the heart.
—Hebrews 4:12, NIV

One of the most powerful weapons we have in our arsenal of growth and developing a safe space within our own head is dialogue—the right words—which builds trust. It allows us to sort the truly trustworthy from the truly malevolent. Learning to divide these things through vulnerable, honest, faithful communication is how we can create a new world after betrayal.

FUNCTIONS CHECK

1. What words do you use to describe other people most often?
2. What behaviors do you find yourself taking that, afterword, you find yourself saying, "That wasn't me?"
3. What is it you're unwilling or scared to feel?
4. What small, tiny step toward that fear can you take today?

CHAPTER 4

CHAOS INOCULATION

THE SAYING "HAIR OF the dog" is the shortened version of "hair from the dog that bit you." It's commonly used in reference to the idea that to cure a hangover, you drink more alcohol. Originally, it came from the belief that a treatment for rabies transmitted through a dog bite was to consume a potion brewed using some of the hair of the dog that bit you.

While the jury's still out on the curative effects of actual dog hairs, the principle of consuming a controlled portion of the thing that originally hurt you is often the best course of action to survive.

It applies to creating antivenoms and vaccines. Antivenoms are made by extracting a small amount of snake venom and injecting it into an envenomated person, thereby allowing antibodies to be generated to mitigate the damaging effects of a snake bite.

The concept of vaccination was first observed and recorded by English physician Edward Jenner in the 18th century. He noticed that dairy maids who contracted cowpox on their hands were far less likely to suffer the effects of smallpox. This is where the first vaccinations came from; even the word vaccination, coined by Jenner in 1796, comes from the Latin word *"vaccinus"* which means, "of the cow."

A controlled dose of something harmful turns out to be the cure, and in some cases, can result in the organism being better off than before. You've heard the term "resiliency" used when it comes to mental health. But what does it mean to become better than you were before an encounter with adversity? Author and statistician Nassim Taleb describes this phenomenon as "antifragility." This describes something which becomes stronger as a result of being partially broken down. The post-traumatic growth idea is an antifragile idea. Most of this book has been concerned with the idea of moral injury instead of trauma. Part of the reason for that is because the word "trauma" is often associated with PTSD, but it is actually relatively uncommon for someone to truly become disordered after having experienced trauma.

Trauma here can be thought of as an overwhelming experience of accelerated chaos, uncertainty, or randomness which results in at least a short-term breakdown of psychological, and sometimes physical, structures. The word itself has its origins with a piercing wound, a type of injury which never quite heals back to the way the body was before. Think Frodo at the end of the original *Lord of the Rings* series. The pain in his pierced shoulder never fully went away.

But trauma and our antifragile nature is part of the story, or else humans would have died off a long time ago. Unfortunately, it has become much easier for the comfort-seeking person to become traumatized because, in part, their environment has not given them the low-does stress to practice with. There was never any "trauma inoculation" to prepare the growing child for what may be to come. That process of initiation became optional as a result of using our technology in service to a story which placed affluence and comfort above sacrifice and beneficial hardship.

Prepare the Child for the Road, Not the Road for the Child.

—Jonathan Haidt

What we consider traumatic today, may have been closer to a daily occurrence to earlier humans. Even turning the clock back about 200 years proves this out, when long stretches without food, poor shelter, sanitation conditions, and dental decay were the norm, not the exception. How did they get along? They were in an environment which allowed the inherent antifragile nature to do its thing. The body was highly adept at confronting extreme randomness. Now, of course, it should be noted that there is a point of extreme stress (responses to uncertainty or levels of randomness, if you like) which results in decay and poor life expectancy. But in the 21st century, we've worked to swing the pendulum in the other direction, with no, or very little uncertainty. And that's not good either. The inability to handle some randomness through our life experiences makes the threshold for perceiving an event as traumatic far lower.

In modernity, these efforts at making things far more certain and controlled has, in many ways, caused more harm than help. It turns out, for example, that a certain amount of temperature fluctuation ends up being much healthier in the long-run than sitting in 72 degrees all the time. Introducing some discontinuity in one's meal plan, i.e. fasting intermittently, turns out to be a great strategy for positive metabolic health rather than consuming food on a forever regular (nonrandom) schedule. Our body's ability to stay mobile throughout our life demands that we put it through low-level stressors that challenge and add randomness to our movements.

When the traumatized human is set within the right ecosystem of low-level stressors, it allows the body and mind to adapt to, and become stronger from, adversity—which today we call "trauma." The body's default state is one of health, and it's a state we are primed at returning to *if* the ecological conditions and the willingness of the heart are set in order. It is by no means a foregone conclusion that a traumatic experience equals a PTSD diagnosis. Indeed, only about 10% of people exposed to a traumatic event end up with a stress disorder. Likely fewer still if the environment they occupy after the event is fully conducive to allowing inside-out healing to occur.

How does this mechanism of beneficial low-level stress work psychologically? Remedies from phobias are illustrative of the phenomena—gazing voluntarily at the thing which "poisons" you makes you stronger.

In the book of Numbers—whose original Hebrew title was *Bamidbar*, or "Into the Wilderness"—one of the rebellion stories describes the introduction of venomous snakes into the Israelite camp. The snakes showed up on account of the people's actions when they willfully turned from the holy to the profane. After enough of the rebels had perished, the people pleaded with Moses for a cure. In chapter 21, verse 8, Yaweh says to Moses, "Make a snake and put it up on a pole; anyone who is bitten can look at it and live."[7]

---

7   The pole here is representative of consecrating a portion of land as sacred. It's a symbolic connection to a higher power which confers a certain divine inhabitation to the land. In ancient times and in many religious frameworks, planting a pole or a pointing-up altar of some sort validates the taking of new land, or denotes the generating of a piece of ordered creation on the otherwise chaotic cosmos.

The principle is that by voluntarily facing the thing you fear (snakes are human's ancient predators and often represent that thing we fear most), you can find your **cure**. In a therapeutic setting, a patient develops courage and competence to face the thing they fear with small "injections" of vaccination in the form of an encounter with the thing they are afraid of. This is called *exposure therapy*. For the agoraphobic (fear of crowds), this might start out with looking at a picture of many people in a room, then slowly progressing to a trip to a less crowded corner shop, and finally to a concert. For them, the "abyss" was all the fear connected to groups of people. By looking at, gazing at, the thing that most frightens them long enough, not only does the fear of crowds diminish, but their confidence in other areas of life improves as well. By becoming stronger in one area, strength becomes generalized as the antifragility effect is allowed to take place.

The process is not intended to remove fear altogether, but to develop courage and to generalize that courage across much broader contexts. Fear, after all, can inform us of where we need to do the work. In *Harry Potter and The Chamber of Secrets*, Harry and Ron must navigate the sewage system in order to find what they were after. And, of course, what is to be found down there? A Basilisk, a dragon-like serpent creature, that can kill just by looking at you. It can really take you out, which is why when Harry ended up getting bit, he was nearly to the point of death before the phoenix intervened. What does Harry receive as his reward for defeating the dragon? The virgin, Ginny (a form of the name Virginia), of course, as so many ancient stories tell. The virgin (and the gold the dragon hides) is symbolic of the greatest prize we could receive after contending with the thing of which we are most afraid. And how does Harry defeat the primary antagonist, Tom Riddle, in that movie? By using the Basilisk tooth, itself. Conquering one monster allows us to conquer many others using pieces of the first. This is post-traumatic growth. This is how we become antifragile, mythologically speaking.

The world is full of venomous, chaotic encounters. What we don't need is a denial of its reality, but a practice to develop the psychological immunization called *courage* in a world full of snakes. We cannot develop this courage in passive isolation and avoidance. This only makes the dragons bigger and more venomous. We have to voluntarily confront small portions of the bigger things that we fear the most in order to master the chaos that lies past the borders of certainty.

Where your fear is, there is your task.
—Carl Jung

In a state of chronic stress which characterizes both PTS and a significant amount of Western living, the common response is to medicate the uncomfortable emotions and physical states with food, drugs, sex, TV…anything to distract and detach us from the pain of experiencing some "hair of the dog." But numbing is effectively the same as isolation; medically supervised numbing could be necessary in some circumstances or for limited amounts of time, but **it is not a cure**.

By attempting to remedy our anxieties, we end up exacerbating the very thing we are trying to avoid. Rather than avoiding pain, it's best to become familiar with pain in small, manageable pieces, so that when a huge dose of pain inevitably comes around, we've done all the prep work to make ourselves resilient in its face.

For example, world-class athletes are able to perform, not because of their abilities to deny the pain of competition altogether, but because of their ability to know precisely what to do with that pain. Pain, or stress, is interpreted as useful information because it has become familiar. Elite performers know the pain but don't mind it; it hasn't turned to suffering even though it's the same objective pain signal the suffering debutante experiences.

The same concept is true for the warfighter. To maintain good form in the heat of battle, the warrior must be fully present and aware of the discomfort. The warrior-athlete does not try to pretend the pain is not there in order to overcome. The warrior-athlete becomes familiar with the pain in order to know exactly how to respond to what the pain and its sensations are telling him or her.

Uncomfortable feelings are supposed to be leveraged as our teachers. We have a choice about what to do with these feelings, how to respond in the face of discomfort, and that choice can make all the difference in our ability to thrive. The path we take in the face of pain determines whether we are taking advantage of our innate antifragility.

A man once went to his psychiatrist to help him deal with all his anxiety. He was a professor and felt like his anxiety was getting in the way of his ability to do his job. The psychiatrist prescribed him Xanax and told him to come back in 30 days. Upon his return, the physician asked, "How is your anxiety today?" To which the man responded, "Well, the anxiety is gone, but there's another problem."

"Oh, and what is that?" asked the psychiatrist.

"While I don't feel as anxious anymore, the stack of papers I need to grade has just been sitting there on my desk, and I really don't care much as to whether or not I grade them."

In his case, it's not obvious that the elimination of the pain of anxiety was a net benefit. In fact, angst may have been a positive coping strategy that propelled him to complete his work. The problem wasn't the anxiety. The problem was framing anxiety as something that needed to be numbed instead of listened to. Maybe the best cure to this man's anxiety was to think of it as an impulse that compelled him to complete his work on time. Often, once meaningful work gets completed, the anxiety goes away on its own because the feeling has done its work.

The buffalo of the great plains have a lesson to teach on how we can handle uncomfortable emotions. When they see a storm approaching, instead of trying to outrun it and thus prolong the amount of time spent under its torrent, they run toward it so that it passes overhead more quickly.

There is a certain inevitability to storms, whether that's attending to work deadlines, family obligations, raising small children, or suffering through yet another live-action Disney remake. While we can't choose for the storms to stop, there is some good news. We do have some agency in which storms we decide to take responsibility for. If we make the choice to engage with a "storm" matching our abilities, a magical thing can happen—we find our flow state.

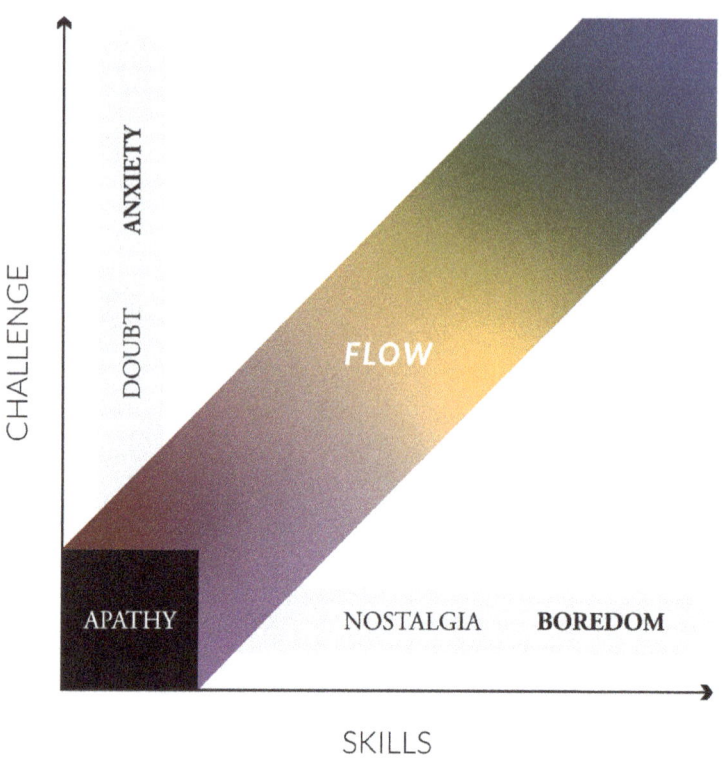

This is a state where the performer becomes fully involved with the activity, where a sense of self dissolves, time fades, and focus is heightened. It's a state where the human creature is acting out the thing they were designed to do in that moment. The professor, assuming he sees his profession as a meaningful endeavor, likely finds himself in a state of flow while teaching or grading papers, but it was the anxiety that served as the initial kick to get him there.

Flowing with a task is a physiological state which is opposite to a state of dread. It's a state we can find ourselves in when we are engaged in something that is optimally meaningful to us. Finding flow is very likely an indicator that we've found a place where our actions and story are in full alignment, an optimal balance of chaos and order, comfort and discomfort—the edge of growth.

Flow is an experience one can achieve playing chess, cooking a meal, navigating a squad-sized field training exercise, writing a book, or racing a triathlon. The course of one's life is figuring out where we stand on that path between our imperfect nature and the perfection we aim toward and finding flow is feedback that we're likely on this path.

This is the experience of hitting the mark discussed in Chapter Two and it's actually possible to measure it physiologically through hormonal and brainwave sensors. How can we go about finding activities to do which enable flow states? We do things, oriented with our bigger stories, we are enthusiastic about. The word "enthusiasm" means, "to be inspired or possessed by the spirit of God," or the spirit of the "highest good" if you prefer. When we are enthusiastic, we are acting out the highest form of what it means to be a creature made out of dirt but which is also made in God's image.

FUNCTIONS CHECK

1. Describe a task or job you've conducted in the past that produced an experience of flow.
2. What actions have you taken in life that felt like they took very little psychological energy to do and left you feeling fulfilled after you'd conducted them?
3. After a good day of work, what sensations occur for you in order to know that you did what you were supposed to do? How do you know you're doing the right thing?
4. What does enthusiasm mean to you?

CHAPTER 5

WHAT MAKES A HERO?

BEFORE OUR UNDERSTANDING OF Modern science, there was a type of protoscience called "Alchemy"—which we briefly examined earlier—forms of which were practiced across the Muslim world, China, and Europe. It was a framework for understanding the natural world. One of the seven principles of Alchemy is that of polarity. This principle states:

> *Everything is dual; everything has poles; everything has its pair of opposites; like and unlike are the same; opposites are identical in nature, but different in degree; extremes meet; all truths are but half-truths; all paradoxes may be reconciled.*

As we are rewriting our stories following moral injury, we might be able to apply this principle here. Part of the path of self-re-invention is to have journeyed through the full range of human emotions. On this idea of polarity, we cannot be happy unless there is such a thing as sadness. Indeed, no human emotion is not without its opposite; that's how they are defined. Isaac Newton was a student of Alchemy and his third law—that for every action, there is an equal and opposite reaction—was certainly influenced by his contemplations on polarity. This principle applies to both domains, physics and feelings.

The challenge in our recovery is trying to understand how the human heart can hold space for emotions that appear to be so opposite to one another. But how we hold the tension between opposites might be our best path to grow that tree to heaven from the roots of hell. The full truth of the story must be able to live with the tension of paradox, and by holding that tension, we grow into our original potential.

There's no such thing as a mountain peak without the valleys in between to provide the summit's relief. The difference between whether we discover the mountain peaks of emotions associated with love, joy, and surprise is how we travel the valley of fear, anger, and sadness.

Resentment, dread, and grief may, in time, prove to be the raw materials of hope, compassion, and joy. But there is a tension between what connects those states— at first, it's not obvious at all how the capacity to hate could be an antecedent for the capacity to love. So let's look at an example.

Consider the emotion of passion. Is it good or bad?

Are villains in superhero movies passionate about what they're up to? Is the hero passionate? If they are both passionate, how do we know who the good guy is?

I think some of the most compelling hero stories are those where the hero doesn't succeed or overcome the challenge due to his or her superior virtuousness, but in spite of it. The best heroes have flaws which they overcome, but maybe those flaws are nec-essary—for if there are no flaws, there's nothing to overcome and there is no story. The more flaws there are to overcome, the more compelling the story—polarity at work. When Superman was first released as a radio program, it quickly became uninteresting because Kryptonite had not yet been introduced. Here you had this bulletproof superhuman with no weaknesses to overcome and no one was interested. It wasn't a good story because it wasn't the human story.

> # The superheroes you have in your mind (idols, icons, titans, billionaires, etc.) are nearly all walking flaws who've maximized one or two strengths.
> —Tim Ferriss

The difference between the passionate villain and passionate hero is the nature of the sacrifice each character makes. The hero sacrifices a part of themselves for the sake of others. The villain sacrifices others for the sake of themselves.

Consider two scenes from *Avengers: Endgame*. In one scene, to acquire an infinity stone that was needed to gain absolute power over the galaxy, a life had to be given in exchange. Thanos chooses to sacrifice Gamora, his adopted daughter, in order to gain this power. Conversely, when Ironman acquires the stones, he chooses instead to sacrifice himself so that others may live, a culmination of all the lessons he learned since the very first movie.

Ironman and Thanos are both passionate about achieving their goals, and in the end, they both get access to the power of the infinity stones—but one operates from a place of sacrifice for the whole while the other operates from sacrifice for only the self. This is the same trope packed into the Cain and Abel story in Genesis

Four. They both sacrificed, but one was found wanting while the other was pleasing.

Our emotions can make good counselors but terrible masters. We must be willing to sacrifice their hold on us to turn them into something else. Transmuting these emotions into something that serves the good is our task. So, what do we do with the tension between passions?

Once again there is good news. The good news is that just because we feel hatred, dread, aggression, anger, spite and such, these emotions in and of themselves don't make us the villain—and could in fact be the very thing needed to realize the heroic side of ourselves. In your anger, do not sin (Eph 4:26). Ironman was arrogant, self-centered, and narcissistic yet still revealed himself to be the central hero of the story because of his willingness, in the end, to sacrifice himself.

Being a hero very often coincides with a fight against being controlled by anger. But that doesn't mean that one is no longer a hero if one feels anger or hatred. Is a father or mother wrong to hate the forces in the world that would corrupt their children? Can a God-fearing priest take up arms to defend his monastery from the Viking hoard? It has everything to do with how these aggressions are harnessed and what they are aimed toward.

The opposite of love is not hate, it's indifference.
—Elie Wiesel

How one holds the tension between anger and love might be the key to understanding how to transform trauma into growth.

Learning how to make the right sacrifices teaches us how to hold this tension. Being good is not the same as being tame. Being good is realizing your capacity for bad but knowing what to do with it. It's the difference between explosive and surgical anger.

**A harmless man is not a good man.
A good man is a very dangerous man
who has that under voluntary control.**
—Jordan Peterson

THE HEROINE'S LOVE

In C.S. Lewis' *The Great Divorce*, there was a mother named Pam, who stood on the doorsteps of Heaven. Her son Michael died at an early age and was waiting for her on the other side. What the mother misunderstood about the whole endeavor of Heaven was that she had to love God more than her son in order to spend eternity with both. She held so tightly to the wrong she experienced when her son died that she was fixated on being with him again at the expense of all other relationships.

This was Pam's response to Heaven.

"Well, when am I going to be allowed to see him?" she asked.

"There's no question of being allowed, Pam. As soon as it's possible for him to see you, of course he will. You need to be thickened up a bit."

"How?" said the Ghost [Pam]. The monosyllable was hard and a little threatening.

111

"I'm afraid the first step is a hard one," said the Spirit [Reginald]. "But after that you'll go on like a house on fire. You will become solid enough for Michael to perceive you when you learn to want someone else besides Michael. I don't say 'more than Michael,' not as a beginning. That will come later. It's only the little germ of a desire for God that we need to start the process."

"Oh, you mean religion and all that sort of thing? This is hardly the moment...and from you, of all people. Well, never mind. I'll do whatever's necessary. What do you want me to do? Come on. The sooner I begin it, the sooner they'll let me see my boy. I'm quite ready."

Pam still doesn't get the physics of Heaven. Reginald tries to explain:

"But, Pam, do think! Don't you see you are not beginning at all as long as you are in that state of mind? You're treating God only as a means to Michael. But the whole thickening treatment consists in learning to want God for His own sake."

She was hateful, bitter, and resentful about the whole affair because she loved her son too much, and what once looked like love and care instead transmuted into jealousy and pride. Her sacrifice had her aiming in the wrong direction. She was trying to sacrifice her son's well-being for her own sake, not sacrificing her understanding for the sake of her son.

The mother's ultimate sacrifice is to let go of their child—when the time comes—to go and explore and contend with a world where the child will most surely be harmed. The mother/child relationship is symbolic here of any relationship a caregiving female has with someone of the community. This care has a huge role to play, but it can turn toxic when dependency starts to creep in. This letting go of the child is the mother's crucifixion, symbolically speaking. That is the virgin Mary's story, depicted most famously in Michelangelo's Madonna della Pietà. The heroine voluntarily sacrifices her role as caregiver and protector to allow the child to escape the confines of the nest so that he or she can mature and become their own versions of heroes and heroines.

Pam was the female villain for not allowing her son (at least in her mind) to completely fulfill his role.

The antagonist in the Rapunzel story, Mother Gother, is an archetype of Pam. She hoarded youth at the expense of Rapunzel by using emotional blackmail to prevent Rapunzel from ever leaving. She posed as a loving mother, but was not willing to make a sacrifice and allow Rapunzel to leave, eventually becoming a devouring, overly protective and tyrannical mother.

The paradigm—the paradox—of Love integrates the potential for pain because it allows the other the freedom to choose. That leaves the door open for catastrophe, betrayal, and broken hearts. That's why true Love is scary and takes an immense amount of courage because it lets the other decide for themselves. The hero and heroine's Love knows the risk and opts for the possibility—but not the guarantee—of a happy ending.

The heart is deceitful above all things, and desperately sick; who can understand it?
—Jeremiah 17:9, ESV

Loving well always involves risk, which means a broken heart may be necessary to start the process of post-traumatic growth as a cocoon must eventually dissolve away to produce a butterfly. And if we can discover that process, our trauma, our moral injury, and the story we occupy starts to find its context, pain will find its polar opposite, and our personal hero's journey can begin to lead us...

Home.

CHAPTER 6

CONSUMPTION

N OW, TO DIVE FURTHER into making the abstract nature of narratives and values more concrete, we will again borrow from another idea from the Alchemists. The most coveted object in the world was thought to be the Philosopher's Stone. This legendary object could bring immortality to the user and turn base, worthless metals into pure gold. If this is sounding familiar from a Harry Potter story you once read, J.K. Rowling took many cues in her storytelling from Alchemical thought. This stone is also considered the "elixir of life," which archetypically, was the thing the hero brought back to their hometown after having completed their adventures.

While of course, no such artifact was ever discovered, we can take this stone idea and apply it psychologically. What is an "object" that could help us transmute base materials of life disappointment, let down, and tragedy into pure gold? Into life after moral injury? It would be something that could carry us through the darkest things the human experience has to offer us.

In order to make these stories and philosophies real in our lives, for the narrative worlds and the concrete world we live in to interact, we must learn what it means to *consume* them. That which we consume, we become—and the nutrients in food are not the only nutrients the human being needs to grow, especially after trauma. We need to be fed by good conversations with our community, good exercise, good thinking...good *content* in order for our souls to be nourished. And if we're going to decide to put our energies toward good content, it means we must sacrifice other content.

> Why do you spend money
> for what is not bread,
> And your wages for what does not satisfy?
> Listen carefully to Me, and eat what is good,
> And let your soul delight itself in abundance.
> —*Isaiah 55:2, NKJV*

It's interesting that we should call it "consuming content" when we refer to reading the news, a book, social media posts, or other visual media. To consume something means "to destroy by separating into parts which cannot be reunited, as by burning or eating." In the ancient Hebrew culture, this was precisely what they were up to with their sacrificial rituals that don't make much sense to us today.

Here is the pattern: something valuable is offered up to be sacrificed, the offering is "passed through" the altar (let's call it a spiritual informing or transforming with meaning), and it's broken it into its constituent pieces through burning. Those pieces are then consumed by the one making the sacrifice and the one doing the consuming is put into a form patterned after the higher ideal. Give up an item or concept, allow it to be transformed by a process that you place your faith in, and then the leftover is assimilated by the one making the offer.

Let's walk through a few examples.

First off, language. The individual dots, crosses, and symbols that compose a letter don't in themselves have any intrinsic meaning. If you've ever been to a foreign country that doesn't use your alphabet, you've experienced what this is like. The arrangement of the individual markings that form letters have no meaning to you. In order for you to gain the understanding of the markings, you have to sacrifice an old way of interpretation. You must surrender yourself to the meaning of a language which you did not create. You don't get to decide what the letters mean, you have to give up your old understanding in order for meaning to overlay the arrangement of the symbols. The "breaking into its constituent pieces through burning" is the learning process. You have to burn off your unwillingness to let go of your old way of seeing things in order to be informed by the new meaning of the strange alphabet. The "passing through" is the process by which otherwise random assortments of lines and curves are given their meaning. Finally, the consumption is the ability to use an alphabet for meaningful communication. The learner adopts this foreign method, assimilating it into their own language, *making the foreign familiar.*

If everyone decided to just go their own way and create their own alphabets, there would be no shared meaning because there would be no sacrifice by individuals to let go of their own private alphabets. There was no offering up, no passing through, no shared consumption for the benefit of all.

This is the pattern I want to invite you to consider as you progress through the second half of this book, as we move from theory and philosophy to practical application. The pattern is to surrender some previously held meaning you hold for things, allow it to be informed by something outside yourself and retooled in a more usable way for you. Hopefully, this idea is already activating what you know about moral injury. A moral injury is this process done involuntarily on a scale too awe-inducing to be able to manage through a normal process of learning. Trauma is kind of like learning too quickly. This is why recovery from trauma and moral injury has everything to do with taking that rupture and applying a sacrificial process—which allows our previous understanding to pass through a bigger meaning, and then be broken up into usable pieces. It has to be done more intentionally than, say, learning Japanese.

Again, there is a faith component to this process, which we will discuss in the next chapter. The reason faith is an essential part of the process is because if you've never experienced that transformation process yourself, and perhaps have only seen it in others, it can be hard to believe it can be true for you as well. You cannot hop into their passenger's seat and experience it first hand unless it is your very own story. The closest we get is watching movies and listening to stories.

In the Hebraic portrayal of sacrifice, there's a very important *exchange* occurring through these rituals. But it's not like a business exchange where there are contracts and an obvious *vis a vis* transaction where you know precisely what you're going to get in return for the money paid. It's more like how your taxes work.

When we pay taxes (or tithe to the church, if you prefer), we offer up a sacrifice—the mechanism that allows us to participate in a bigger thing—the money passes through the elected officials' office, and the result (if the system isn't plagued with corruption, of course) is a well-maintained infrastructure that everyone is able to "consume," an infrastructure that might not be possible if everyone were simply acting according to their private interests. You, as the taxpayer, didn't exactly make that exchange in the same way as shopping at the store. There had to be a level of trust along the way that the governing body would be responsible with your hard earned money and operate in the best interest of those they serve. When the governing body loses that trust, it begins to fail. Historically, governing offices were judged based on how well they embodied a higher transcendent authority for this reason. The temptation to take personal advantage of these sacrifices is always there, which is why kings and rulers had to, themselves, give an account to an even higher, perfect power, lest they, too, become corrupt. Members of a population can themselves be morally injured when they run into the corruption of a sacrificial system gone horribly wrong.

This step of faith and trust is the difference between an economic one-for-one transfer and a sacrificial trust-based exchange. Transactions are known, certain, and unambiguous. They don't require much trust and faith because the market has provided clearcut expectations on how that works. A faith-based exchange means you surrender your right to your private interests and in return, at some unknown future point, you are rewarded with that which you most need to consume. It's what allows you to be transformed into something more than you were before.

The ancient idea of the food sacrifice is that by consuming food that has first been presented back up to Heaven, the highest ideal, or a bigger meaning, the one consuming the food is now informed by that which the plants or animal has passed through. The body of the person is being set into a pattern by the thing consumed. At this level of analysis, we're not looking at this through a nutritional lens, per se, but the spiritual realities which the ritual embodied. These people were aiming to embody spiritual principles by the things they consumed through a process of sacrifice. This is partially the point of eating a kosher diet. Anything not kosher was considered a foreign and toxic *pattern*, something unholy and unfit for the ancient Hebrews to consume.

You may be asking, so what? What does lamb killing by ancient peoples have to do with me? These days, we don't offer up animals like that, and we have a difficult time relating to spiritual realities in light of 21st century materialism. But this process is still very much alive and well. Scientists must sacrifice spending resources on investigating one thing in order to investigate another. A value set must be overlayed with the scientific process because there are an infinite number of things to investigate. How do you decide what to prioritize? The process must be passed through a framework of perception and a value judgment rendered. Prioritizing means placing higher meaning on one thing over another and this is in accord with a value structure, a story, which informs the consumption process.

Here's how we model this same pattern every day with the messages we allow ourselves to receive through various mediums (i.e. "media," which is the plural for "medium"). A *medium* is a means by which two things are channeled from one to another. A mediator is an entity which facilities exchanges between two parts. In the ancient Hebrew conception, humanity is the mediator between that which is above and that which is below, between the principles of heaven and the form of earth. It's humanity's job to form material (the "what") to shape with the forms of spiritual realities (the "so what"). The means for this mediation are through once again, sacrifice, a passing through, and consumption and integration. It's just like the chess game—a board is composed of material objects and the mediator, the rule maker, overlays the pieces with meaning, allowing the game to be played. This means that to play a game, one must voluntarily restrict oneself to the rules.

We integrate the patterns of that which is consumed into who we are becoming. The behavior of the body is patterned after the information passed down by the head or mind. When we play chess, we sacrifice our desire to flip the table and use the pieces like ammunition to be hurled at our annoying younger brother so that we can play a mutually beneficial game with another person. To sacrifice here is to allow our behavior to be subject to the rules, and the consumption is the ability to play well with others in an ordered manner. When two people subject themselves to an agreed upon rule set, it opens the door to participating in a peaceful experience with one another, even if it has to start with a bit of friction.

By voluntary participation in a rule set that we place our faith in, we are consuming micro stories of peace.

This sacrificial exchange also works with how we engage in conflict in relationships. Maybe we'd rather keep well enough alone in our marriages, for example, and even though there might be a bit of resentment building, maybe the devil you know is better than the one you don't. We become afraid, or even petrified, of making even one critical remark about the other person's behavior, as we're afraid that the integrity of the relationship is in jeopardy because perhaps it cannot survive an honest look at its deficiencies. Why?

It's likely because when we were much younger, we were taught that if we ask someone to take our needs seriously, we would be dismissed or abandoned by our caregivers. At that age, abandonment basically means death. We learn to keep quiet so that we don't lose out on an attachment to a parent; in anxious or avoidant-type relationships, that comes at the expense of our voice. Eventually, this story—the one that tells us that it's better to keep quiet than to have hard conversations or else we'll be abandoned—lived out long enough will turn monstrous.

We might conceive of difficulties in a marriage like the mythological creature Medusa. What were her characteristics? Anyone who dared to gaze directly at her was petrified. She had hundreds of venomous snakes around the crown of her head. How is she defeated? By allowing her to see her reflection. What does a reflection do? It gives the gorgon an identity. It labels what the monster is so that it can be de-monstered into usable pieces—whose head can then be cut off and used against future enemies.

You make the sacrifice to voluntarily engage in constructive conflict, and that is done as an act of courage, because that's what it takes to confront monsters. The alternative is that you stay petrified by the multi-snaked creature that is the looming dialogue you'd prefer to avoid with your husband or wife. (Guys, your wife is not the Medusa here. It's the conversation you don't want to have that's the monster.) You first label with as much precision and honesty as possible what the problem is and how the exchange will be conducted—establish what both of you want as an end result of the conflict. Reflection. You cut it to pieces with your constructive dialogue. If done successfully, you've offered up short-term comfort for a bit of conflict. An old way of relating must be burned off, and in exchange, you receive an updated relationship that is now better informed and two people who are now more integrated. Repeat as needed.

A person's success in life can usually be measured by the number of uncomfortable conversations he or she is willing to have.
—Tim Ferriss

When I was first learning how to do a front flip off a diving board, I stood there at the edge, looking down into the thing I feared. I was frozen and couldn't get myself to move. My brother, who had already mastered the task, urged me on again and again, showing me how to do it. At last, I mustered my courage and went for it. Success! Then the very next one was fun. The fear faded when I at last confronted it and took on the experience of my own accord. Then the task transformed into a pursuit of mastery. That's what having uncomfortable conversations is like. Too many of us are taught to avoid them, or aren't taught how to engage in them in a healthy way.

The way out of these unhealthy attachments is to first of all, become aware of the pattern, then practice a new kind of pattern which allows both parties to fight constructively, without fear of the other leaving. It's a series of small sacrifices which allow you to consume the beneficial byproduct of fair fighting. We must learn to become honest about our anxiety with one another, and we find out quite rapidly that many others are feeling the exact same way and are in fact relieved that someone has finally put words to an otherwise unspoken reality.

* * *

Sacrifices which place spiritual truths ahead of ego-needs provide the fuel we need to contend with the realities of a trauma-laden, chaotic world. What is fuel for the soul, the elixir of life? It's whatever connects us to a story that is greater than the realities of trauma. What, then, does the soul need to consume, precisely?

The type of content our souls need to move forward in our stories is the wisdom found in the pages, images, and conversations of repeatedly told across history. These behave as mediums to communicate the story in a way the listener can understand. We then take apart the story and extract useful pieces of information which we can then integrate for the future. That's what information is: it's something which puts a thing "into form." It should be emphasized again that we integrate useful pieces of the stories we experience, not necessarily the whole thing all at once. Different stories highlight different aspects of the human journey. There will always be portions of epic narratives that resonate more than others. You might consume and reflect on that which compels your attention, and discard the rest.

When someone allows themselves to be subjected to a higher ideal, or the rules, the spirit of the ideal is informing the body how to operate. When constrained to the playing of the game, the mind is driving the body to obey. By paying taxes, some proportion of life force in the form of money is subjected to the greater needs of the population (ideally). In a marriage, the proper way to be in form is for both parties to subject themselves to a higher ideal, the relationship itself.

However, the direction of influence can run the other way when we are not willing to sacrifice the influence of our ego. This is how this process goes wrong, when the rules run bottom up, ego to spirit, instead of top down, spirit to ego. An ego-driven life is one where the body puts the mind into form, the flesh puts the spirit into its pattern, rather than the higher ideal of the spirit putting the flesh into its pattern.

You might wonder, why is it we must rely on external stories to drive our own? Why can't we chart our own path, generate a story from whole cloth that's all ours? Am I not the master of my own destiny? While a major cultural influence in the 21st century is to "find your truth," or to just, "be your own true self," I'm afraid such self-centered philosophies cannot work long term because we only get to know ourselves in relationship to other people. Our stories must negotiate with others.

I think it's partly for the same reason that the eye cannot see itself. It might look in a mirror and see a reflection, but that's not the same thing as the eyeball itself. We were designed to know ourselves by reflecting off each other. Well socialized children have passed through a process of acting out in certain ways, receiving feedback from their peers, and adjusting their behavior in order to play in greater accord by a set of unwritten rules which ultimately facilitate peace (if only until snack time). The reason we can't generate our stories from whole cloth is because there is more than one of us. Sure, the manner in which we act out a bigger story has its uniqueness—there is only one of you born to your family in your location at a certain point in history—but there is also a collective narrative that we all have a duty to both contribute to and be informed by. These are the archetypes. This is the story of Love— unity and peace among a multiplicity. That's the grand narrative.

How do we come to know the details and practicalities of this grand narrative? Well, we look at stories that have persisted for the longest duration of human history. Those that we deem worthy of retelling, we might consider the "meta narratives" of this whole human drama of which we are a part. In a religious setting, you may have heard of this referred to as "canon." It's the same idea. The true human story is the story that has resisted time's decay. There's a reason that Marvel revived Thor from his Nordic roots some 1200 years old. There was some component of that story that rung true enough to spend millions of dollars retelling.

To appreciate the significance of stories, just consider how impactful a cultural classic on the silver screen is. When a large group of people pass through the theater to consume a story, behavior and attitudes can be collectively influenced because we all agree to some extent that what we watched on the screen is describing how life outside the theater actually is. It's the same reason children and cosplayers put on the capes and masks of their favorite heroes; they want to be put into the form of a higher ideal and act that out. Not in a pretend way, but in actuality. We desire to live out stories which reflect the human drama. It allows us to feel connected to something ultimately meaningful and important. Of this, Carl Jung said, "Everybody acts out a myth, but very few people know what their myth is. And you should know what your myth is because it might be a tragedy and maybe you don't want it to be."

When we decide to watch a story with these archetypal patterns, it turns out we are watching parts of *our* story, and perhaps the stories that you are the most interested in ought to be the ones worthy of deeper investigation. Maybe our deepest instinct is the one which draws us to the best stories. By consuming and integrating those stories, we embody the morals those stories have been attempting to tell throughout human history. And when we embody those morals, we are also contributing to that story and giving it new life. Every person in every generation has a part to play, and it may be that in the rapid pace of the 21st century that that story is in need of revivification more than ever, and you're up to bat.

We consume stories to find out what our myth is because it provides us with the psychological fuel to keep us moving forward after experiencing trauma. Ultimately, the human, in order to thrive in a broken world, must be fed the right stories. King Olaf, in *The Vikings* TV series, when questioned about his decisions to go to war, referred to their mythology. One of his opponents protested, "Those are just stories," to which the king responded, "Stories are all we have."

Stories are the load bearers of the weight of life. The weightier life is, the stronger the story must be.

CHAPTER 7

MAKING IT REAL

Trauma gives you two lives.
—Magnus Johnson

WHERE DOES THE RUBBER meet the road when translating thoughts and stories into actions? Any created material thing was once a thought in someone's mind. An inventor may see a fully formed final product in their head, but it is not yet existent in concrete reality. To transform this thought into a tangible thing, the inventor must take action with communication and with behaviors.

Having thoughts is not the same as consuming thoughts, as watching items float down a stream is not the same as jumping in and grabbing those items to add to your collection. To consume a thought means we agree with it or even identify with it. We've fished out a thought from the consciousness stream and made it ours instead of just observing it. Once we agree with a thought, consume a thought, we have an emotional response to whatever the thought means to us. Emotional responses in the body are mediated by the limbic system in the brain. Effectively, this system turns consumed thoughts into chemicals which then affects cellular activity.

This means that if we consume and agree with bad thought content, our cells will respond and adapt to a negative internal environment. We can think ourselves well or think ourselves sick in the right circumstances. These are the placebo and nocebo effects, respectively. When we perceive our outer world is a safe environment for healing, those consumed thoughts can speed a recovery process. If a child receives a kiss and a Spongebob band-aid from his mom, his pain experience of the ouchie changes compared to the kid who had the same injury but no immediate parental care. We create "external" environments for our cells by feeding our insides with our consumed thoughts.

We might define consumption again, in this light, as a transference of things from the mind into the body. The words we give our body to feed on make us well or ill.

Now the brain and nervous system fire off thoughts in the mind for us to contend with, and while we don't have direct control over the mechanism of thoughts popping into our head, we can cultivate an internal posture where the odds of thoughts which disturb us popping into our head are decreased and the odds of us agreeing with those thoughts decrease greater still. This is the idea Cognitive Behavior Therapy is partially based off. If we have recurring, unpleasant, and disruptive thoughts, we can learn to contend with those thoughts with our own disputations of them, or, as we're about to see, learn to let them pass without allowing them to land.

Sometimes these thoughts arise from unfinished business that our Monkey Mind wants us to take care of. This could be as routine as the unfinished business of putting food in your empty stomach or as serious as unresolved childhood trauma. If we still have unfinished business from the past, that chronic signal ends up in the body, and manifests as altered genetic expression due to the hormones and neurotransmission that are affected by these consuming Monkey Mind thoughts. Our bodies in adulthood can suffer from what we experienced as a child if we are not equipped properly to grow from it.

One important characteristic to know about the Monkey Mind is that it has an extremely short-term memory when it comes to neutral and positive life events, and an extremely vivid, long-term memory when it comes to events we perceive as threatening. Its job is to allay threats.

That means if we only consume the thoughts our Monkey Mind produces, we get stuck in threat detection mode and can be blind to all the good that is around us every day. To make equanimity—a state of evenness of temper, especially in difficult times—our new default requires a dedicated practice that we engage in every day. The Monkey Mind will always be there, which means our practice cannot stop. To subordinate and order the thoughts of the Monkey Mind, we must practice the art of awareness. The thoughts coming from that part of us need to have a home, need to be informed of where to go, or else we begin to identify with that inner protector instead of simply taking its opinion as one of many that we could chose to listen to, or not.

That doesn't mean the objective is to never feel uncomfortable emotions. It means that when those uncomfortable emotions do arrive, as they inevitably will, we know what to do with them. We are not consumed by them. Maintaining one's composure while experiencing sadness or anger are not mutually exclusive states of being.

If we only consume bad thought content, our mental chatter only gets worse. We're feeding the Monkey extra fuel to produce disturbing thoughts. We're giving extra ammunition to our internal threat detectors, greatly increasing the chance of experiencing intrusive thoughts.

Don't we have enough to worry about without adding the gasoline of chronic negative news feeds, toxic relationship arrangements, and rumination on past events we have no control over?

Post-traumatic stress, or a state where we're having a tough time of processing a moral injury, might be conceptualized as a Monkey Mind that is completely stuck in threat detection mode. The nervous system has learned to largely distrust the outside world, past a healthy threshold, and needs to relearn which threats are worthy of a stress response, and which are not. This is one of several ways to think about recovery from chronic stress—learning to correctly tag stimuli in our world as safe or unsafe—and the components discussed here all lead to taming that emergency response system, thus lowering the tide on that unending flow of negativity.

These components are:

1. *Meditation* increases our ability to distinguish between the chatter and our conscious thinking. It draws a more coherent line between the observing mind and the Monkey Mind.

2. *Acceptance and forgiveness* help extinguish the bitter flames of unfinished business from the past.

3. *Gratitude* identifies the good and increases our ability to make the good stick instead of defaulting to the bad.

4. *Dialogue* with our internal "parts" facilitates a better relationship between the ego, the observer, and our memories.

5. *Meaningful work* is a physical action which reminds the mind and body that one has the agency and ability to act out in the world and that one's actions are not in vain.

Let us discuss each in turn.

MEDITATION

The word "meditate" means both to become familiar with and to softly repeat to oneself. The former meaning is derived from the Sanskrit tradition while the latter is the use of meditation in the Hebrew Bible. Meditation is a practice of becoming familiar by a soft repetition of repeatedly drawing our awareness to something solid and consistent—an anchor. Sometimes, this anchor can be a passage from a sacred text that we want to learn to embody, or perhaps it's something that keeps us connected to a reality that can easily be forgotten when we are so distracted by modern demands on our attention.

The primary purpose of meditation is to become conscious of, and familiar with, our inner life. The ultimate purpose is to reach the source of life and consciousness.

—Nisargadatta Maharaj

Trauma, in particular, has a way of keeping us from making contact with present-tense realities, creating barriers between the peace that is available in the moment and past recollections of emotionally charged scenarios. The threat detector may still be sounding the alarm for an event that is no longer happening in physical reality but is happening in the mind. As we already learned, what happens in the mind is translated to chemicals in the body in response to perception. As far as our cells are concerned, there is no distinction between the perceptions in the mind and the external world the cell needs to respond to. Most cells that drive our health don't have direct contact with the outside world. Their communication, and thus their functions, are driven by messages that come from a fallible nervous system. The question is, then, what are our minds consuming and feeding into that system, and what do we do if there is something stuck there from a charged event that happened a long time ago?

If a past memory has not been consolidated in the mind, if the memory has not become familiar, accepted, forgiven, covered with gratitude, and been assimilated through dialogue, our internal ego defenses will remind us that the old event is still happening—or at least still has the same meaning and significance as it did when it first occurred. The body responds with stress hormones in response to what the mind tells it. Without repeated cycles of awareness, for all intents and purposes, that event *is* happening in the present—trauma keeps the mind and body literally trapped in a past event.

In that light, trauma recovery through an awareness practice might be considered something like time travel, updating the mind's responses from a past event to responding to the present moment. The type of fear stirred up by recalling emotionally charged memories—as opposed to useful fear in a seriously threatening moment—can be thought of as "False Evidence Appearing Real." FEAR. A meditation practice, over time, helps the mind make the distinction between true and false evidence.

The mind can have a hard time distinguishing between fear sensations in the body—responses like elevated heart rate or sweating palms—and perceptions of the external environment. Mindfulness is the practice of recognizing the associations our thoughts and bodies are having to the environment such that we can regain conscious, top-down control of those unpleasant sensations that seem to pop up automatically.

Much of trauma recovery is a matter of aligning our mental and physical responses to events occurring in the present, rather than responding to the threat detector's false flags. Put another way, it's a process of directing our internal observer at the proper targets so that we do not continually miss the mark. Developing awareness means developing the awareness between activating events, internal interpretations, and the following behaviors. Awareness practices strengthen our ability to observe and respond, rather than sense and react.

How might this work mechanistically? Inside each of us is an observer. This observer cannot be measured scientifically, but has profound effects on the material world. Quantum physics actually has something to say here about this observer. The famous double-slit experiment shows us just how much we don't know about how the human observer affects the material world. What was shown in the experiment was that when just one variable was changed—the presence of someone watching—electrons would behave differently. They set up the experiment in a bunch of different ways and the result was the same: matter is affected by observation alone.

What we give our attention to literally shapes the brain and shapes the world. The **shifting of attention in and of itself** allows us to consolidate memories, reroute maladaptive thoughts, and affect our emotional and behavioral outputs.

In the lobby of a dentist's office I visited recently, there was a unique coffee table unlike any I'd ever seen. It was circular and had a top pane of glass. Underneath was a bed of sand, and a ball bearing was moving around the sand making patterns with swirls and stripes. The ball gave the appearance of moving all by itself as it made these shapes—though there was an unseen magnet below guiding its path.

This is how our observer shapes the brain. The path it takes leaves a neural trail, and the more times it goes down that path, the deeper the impression it leaves on the "sand." The influence that guides its path is invisible, but nonetheless shapes the pattern of the ball.

Our Monkey Mind can have a heavy influence on where the observer goes and the shape in the sand of the brain. Again, the Monkey Mind, the internal watchtower, need not always be dismissed, but we need to understand its nature such that the observer can tell the difference between its signals and our higher order signals. These two can be thought of as a rider on his horse, the former being our observing mind and the latter the Monkey Mind. The inclinations of the internal alarm system are extremely powerful as they are set up to keep us alive against many possible conceivable threats. The horse is stronger than the rider. Now, the rider can have one of three relationships with the horse. He can hang on for dear life as the threat detector goes this way and that, reacting to any type of environmental cue that could possibly be considered threatening. He could resist the horse, and pull as hard as he can one way or the other, hoping that by sheer determination or will power he can dominate and overcome the beast. Or finally, he can learn to work in harmony with the creature, realizing its strength but also realizing that there can be a healthy two-way street between these influences.

One more analogy and we'll get into some application.

Our respiratory system has some very curious neural wiring—it happens automatically in the background as most of us (although

I cannot vouch for everyone) don't have to constantly call to mind the command of "inhale" and "exhale" for it to happen. However, in an instant, we can take conscious control over the flow of air in and out of the lungs. We can either observe the breath and influence its activity or allow it to continue without our awareness. But, like the horse, we cannot hope to have a productive go at the exercise if we resist it entirely and insist that we don't need to breathe. The breath will march on no matter how much the rider tugs at the reins, however, the two can learn to operate with coherence.

The example of our breathing serves both as a metaphor of how different systems influence, and are influenced by, our focal point of attention—and as a practical tool in and of itself to practice this art. For the horse and rider to communicate well, the rider (observing mind) must practice becoming aware of their relationship with the horse, drawing attention to the nature of the connection.

It might not seem like anything is really "happening" if you just sit there and take conscious control of your breathing. Perhaps you have tried meditation before and were left wondering whether anything significant is really going on. But like the ball bearing on the sand, one pass of the little sphere over the sand isn't going to change the total picture in the sand much. However, with enough reps, the whole display can change shape, which means the method by which the mind processes information begins to adjust, ever so slightly, one rep at a time. It's a bit like hair growth, it's only very noticeable in retrospect, but not day-by-day. How long does it take, then? Research has shown that about three weeks of dedicated practice, lasting about 20 minutes per day, is enough to see noticeable changes in brain structure as a result of a mindfulness practice.

A single rep of awareness is to observe something happening in the present moment, something we can refer to as an anchor. A round of meditation involves the presence of a natural distraction for our focus followed by a deliberate refocusing on a still point. *Refocusing after distraction is the process of mediation, not an indication that you're doing it wrong.* As we practice this, we can learn to more seamlessly enter into that flow state discussed previously, as flow is when the observer is fully focused on moment-to-moment phenomena.

Between stimulus and response there is a space. In that space is our power to choose our response. In our response lies our growth and our freedom.
—Victor Frankl

We can expand the space between outside stimuli and internal response with these "reps" of present moment awareness on an anchor. This rep could be conducted either during a formal meditative session or during a 10 second break from your daily business—drawing focus on one sensation, the space between your fingers, the texture of your shirt against your stomach, or the coolness from the A/C.

The breath is considered the most accessible form of anchor. You can get a "rep" of awareness in simply by sensing air moving in and out of your lungs. You're practicing a state of being that is not focused on past worries or future fears, but a state that is only concerned with the now.

Elite warriors are highly mindful individuals, who, even though they may or may not have conducted deliberate breath awareness exercises, have practiced the global skill of awareness and drawing focus to the present in all their training. A warrior is trained not to have knee-jerk reactions to encounters with the enemy. Rather, the warrior is able to scan, perceive, and make rapid decisions based on an assessment of the situation. The warrior has a productive space between stimulus and response so that their actions on the battlefield are precise as they can be. This process is captured in the OODA loop tool, a rapid decision-making technique taught to many service members. This is the observe, orient, decide, act pattern of quick but deliberate decision making.

This is a tool you can practice every day. This idea is also captured in the distress tolerance module of Dialectical Behavior Therapy using the acronym REST: Relax, Evaluate, Set an Intention, Take action. When you're in a situation where you find your emotions rising out of proportion for a situation, pause and remember one of these acronyms, and practice, practice, practice until the acronym is no longer needed and it becomes part of your mode of operating.

Practicing awareness on a present tense anchor allows us to flow through the OODA loop instead of being enslaved to an immediate reaction to an unfavorable stimulus. The elite warrior is primed to think through problems, evaluate solutions, consider risks of various courses of action, and then act decisively. Chronic stress tends to dissolve the steps of orienting and deciding and gets us stuck in an observe/act flash-bang pattern that betrays our intentions in a situation.

In states of chronic stress, the lines between the flash (stimulus), and bang (emotional experience and fallout) can blur into a single sort of event, leaving us confused and frustrated as to why things keep blowing up out of control. As we practice awareness, we can come to learn where those lines are. Specifically, we can learn to describe the specific event that precipitated an emotional response, our own interpretations of the event (what charge of meaning did we choose to place on it), the here and now of experiencing the immediate aftermath of the emotional response, what behaviors we use to express that response, and finally, the aftereffects of that behavior.

FUNCTIONS CHECK

It may be helpful to write out all five features for yourself when considering a time when a response to a situation proved unusual and frustrating.

1. What was the activating event?
2. What was the interpretation of the event's meaning?
3. What was the internal experience of the emotion, including physical sensations?
4. How was that feeling translated into a behavior?
5. How did that emotion influence your functioning the rest of the day?

For an easy way to practice your awareness skill, take a few moments to identify:

1. Five things you can see.
2. Four things you can feel.
3. Three things you can hear.
4. Two things you can smell.
5. One thing you can taste.

Before a demanding day, take a few minutes to conduct the OODA loop or REST tool.

1. Observe: What is my body feeling like? How would I rate my stress level at this moment? Don't take action to change it, just label it exactly as it is and let that be what it will be.

2. Orient: What is the most important thing that needs my attention today? What is going to get in the way of that attention over the course of the day?
3. Decide: What are the very first, second, and third actions to take in service to the most important thing? What do you need to do to eliminate distractions from that one thing?
4. Act: Take the first step.

> "Let me tell you one story here, of a samurai warrior, a Japanese warrior, who had the duty to avenge the murder of his overlord. And he actually, after some time, found and cornered the man who had murdered his overlord. And he was about to deal with him with his samurai sword, when this man in the corner, in the passion of terror, spat in his face. And the samurai sheathed the sword and walked away. Why did he do that?"
>
> "Why?" asked Bill.
>
> "Because he was made angry, and if he had killed that man then, it would have been a personal act, of another kind of act, that's not what he had come to do."

ACCEPTANCE AND FORGIVENESS

These two concepts are often misunderstood as condoning bad behavior and rolling over in the face of a persecutor. In other words, acceptance is misunderstood as labeling a wrong as not so bad, and forgiveness is misunderstood as giving a perpetrator a free pass to continue to cause harm. Those, it turns out, are the opposite of what these actually mean.

Acceptance has a lot to do with being able to hold two truths at once. We can get ourselves in a cognitive rut when we see the world as composed of black and white. One reason we might find ourselves with this internal program is that this type of thinking may be useful in immediate responses to danger—lion equals threat, therefore, run! In extreme, life-threatening circumstances, there is a black and white decision to be made so that one does not get eaten. But applying this type of thinking to the day-to-day becomes "maladaptive." We can even become addicted to the sensations of responding to a crisis because life and our decisions have taught our nervous systems that a perpetual state of crisis is the norm, and we begin to think, if only subconsciously, that it's only during an intense period of crisis where we actually receive the connection, love, and attention we are craving. It's possible, then, to fall into this state where we come to believe that the only way to get our needs met is by manufacturing a crisis. We can have a hard time understanding that if we allow ourselves to be open about our anxieties, fears, and preferences, this is the much more sustainable and healthy path to getting our needs met in relationships. It's possible, though, if we are still working on returning to a healthier way of being, that the option to be open and honest with the people we trust feels more threatening than the status quo.

A survival, black and white perspective can become the default; trauma can leave us with little room for thinking in nuance. Acceptance is the process of allowing nuance back into the picture. In the functions check at the end of this section, there are 10 different examples of what that type of survival thinking looks like. Becoming aware of these allows us to identify more and more often when those thinking patterns arise, so that we can create a distance between the thinking mode and our executive, higher functioning minds.

Acceptance is a step toward taking a more sophisticated view of a past event—and what that means about who we are and how we fit in the world now. We have to come to terms with the reality that much of life is a paradox. Maybe you did make a mistake. Maybe there was something you did to contribute to whatever happened. But maybe it is also true that you were doing the best you could, all things considered. Maybe you did violate your moral code, but given all the nuances and complexities of the situation, perhaps that was the only good—or less bad—choice you had.

When we're immature psychologically, we don't so much need a grown-up view of the world, because, ideally, children are able to play in a relatively safe and predictable environment. There is almost always a parent around to administer justice in the world of lollipops and LEGO sets. And it's perfectly wonderful that children can occupy a space like this in order to grow up in. They are not ready for the nuance of ethical dilemmas.

However, when we grow up, we must dispense with childish ways of thinking. It doesn't mean they were bad, it just means they're not appropriate anymore. The alternative is to become like Peter Pan, king of the lost boys. Pan didn't want to grow up because he saw a negative example of the adults around him and thought, "I never want to be that way." Captain Hook was a bitter, resentful man that could not accept his own mortality. Time had already taken a piece of him (his hand by the crocodile with the clock in its stomach), and he spent his adult years ruling like a tyrant in an attempt to conquer time. And that was not the future Pan wanted. The irony is that the very thing Hook was trying so hard to avoid was the thing that ended up devouring him prematurely.

Both Pan and Hook in this story were contending with the same thing, and both had bad responses—stay immature forever or become a controlling monster. You can choose either path, too. Classic stories are meant to demonstrate the many choices individuals have; each character represents a part of one viewer. The two paths in question for our main characters both lead them away from the real world and into one that cannot last. A Neverland.

Accepting means that our old ways of operating in the world, our less mature versions, cannot sustain us against the realities of tragedy. We have to sacrifice that most precious thing of childhood innocence *and* we must sacrifice our need to conquer our temporality. Otherwise, we are either consumed by an insatiable desire for a substitute form of pleasure and intimacy (Tinker Bell), or are consumed by the dragon (or crocodile) of time before…well, our time.

This means we're also accepting that what we once thought to be a future possibility is now dead. Thus, grief also becomes an important part of acceptance. Something that can get in the way of this process is drowning out the need to grieve with distracting habits. Grief cannot do its work if we are constantly numb.

This can be an overlooked component to giving up old habits. As an example, society tends to think of smoking, taking illicit drugs, and drinking as societal ills and nothing more. For the person working to rid him or herself from such things, it's typically not a simple matter of agreeing with this prognosis and quitting then and there. Those substances provided a type of good to the person consuming them. Why else consume them unless there was some sort of payoff? The negative effects of these things are delayed, and in the moment, provide a sense of comfort and stability. Who doesn't want that?

Of course, we know that these things aren't a long-term strategy, and that there are more sustainable sources from which to find that stability and comfort. You don't often hear someone talking about a positive change in their lives happening as soon as they picked up drinking. However, to quit involves a letting go of a thing that at one point brought a sense of immediate relief. Moving on from that is almost like saying goodbye to a friend, and, indeed, if drinking was done in a group of people we feel comfortable with, we may actually have to say goodbye to actual people.

While working out a moral injury and quitting substance dependence aren't quite the same thing, the need to mourn something lost may still be there in both cases. Accepting involves a sacrifice, and sometimes that comes with the necessity to grieve.

We tend to assume that a scenario involving the choice between the "lesser of two evils" is the exception, when in our broken world, it is the norm and clear-cut moral decisions are the precious exceptions.

To use a very personal example, I was once married in a partnership that I was certain was going to last a lifetime. Sure, I was pretty naive getting into the relationship and didn't ask all the right questions before making that commitment—indeed, I wasn't even conscious of what it was I needed to ask, exactly—but never would I ever have supposed that my then spouse had the capacity to step outside of her initial vows, breaking the marriage apart a few years later.

I was separated for fourteen months in the hopes that the marriage would be restored somehow. My adolescent framework of what marriage was, and the decisions people were capable of making, was not adequate to deal with the current situation. It took the better part of a year and a half to finally accept that divorce, in this case, was the better choice. I had to choose between lesser goods and the reality of making that decision was one of the most painful I ever had to deal with. But making this decision and sacrificing my old way of being was now 100% my responsibility. It did me no good to blame anyone else for the response to the situation in which I now found myself. In struggling with that ordeal, I was compelled to author my first book, *No Less Faithful: How the Scars of Divorce Reveal the Heart of God* in hopes that it would help others in a similar situation.

> **Just because something's not your fault doesn't mean it's not your responsibility. Our ability to act and change is proportional to the amount of responsibility we take on ourselves.**
> —*Mark Manson*

There were many temptations to blame everything on myself—how odd it is that the psyche allows so easily the opportunity to self-deprecate to no end—but I had to learn to accept two truths at once. I did the best I could, *and* I was more naive than I imagined. I tried my best *and* I lost my marriage. I could keep my faith *and* sign a legal document of divorce without violating my conscience in this case.

If our favorite pet, God forbid, is hit by a car and it survives—but only just—a dignified death for the poor creature might be our best, most loving option. That doesn't make the owner a bad person or the world a meaningless place. It just means the owner has allowed themselves to be an agent of a love that looks much more messy than a Christmas morning.

Mercy can be severe

One of the most profound things Captain Jean-Luc Picard ever said gets right at the core of what acceptance is about: "It is possible to make no mistakes and still lose. That is not a weakness. That is life."

In Norse mythology, there is a character named Fenrir. He is a giant wolf which represents the inevitability of the world's destruction. The idea of the world's end was a prominent feature in their stories. And yet, the will to fight despite knowing that all may be lost still pervades the Viking's psyche. You stay in the fight despite knowing that the odds are heavily stacked against you, and you fight like it's the last thing you'll ever do.

And the better we can accept that the odds are against us, the better warriors we become, because failure no longer stands as a judgment against our effort, character, or personal constitution. Rather failure is a thing in this world that happens for us in order to change us to who we are meant to become. Recovery from failure turns us into stronger humans as pruning in winter allows a greater harvest in the fall.

Failure is technically defined as a "nonperformance of something due." We think of it as something gone irrevocably wrong, something that has caused decay, or some permanence of an end to things. But as Captain Picard points out, failure is a part of life, it's information. The desolation of Fenrir is part of the deal.

But what about that definition above? Is it wrong? Think of it like this—there are two stages of failure. The first is an inevitable component of being human. The second is where we get to exercise our free will and make something out of the first.

The first stage happens simply as a result of existing in a fallen world. Abuse, a combat mission gone wrong, communication breakdown—there are a thousand examples of how our symbolic giant wolf inevitably tears our world apart. Maybe we played a hand in it out of ignorance or maybe, like a small child in an abusive family, we were merely thrown into this brokenness. But this first failure is inevitable. The Northmen got that one right.

The second stage is what we decide to do with that failure. In the Adam and Eve story, it might well be that the first real failure, the moment of The Fall, was the moment Adam blamed the woman for his misgivings. God told them not to eat of the tree knowing full well they would. If you've ever raised a toddler, you know that the instant you tell them not to reach into the cookie jar, they're going to reach into the cookie jar.

Human's evolution into a self-conscious state is inevitable. This self-consciousness fell upon Adam and Eve as soon as they ate of the forbidden fruit. Their error was a result of their immaturity and the deception by the serpent. You might even say they didn't know any better, because for all intents and purposes, there were still unconscious children.

Notice God's initial reaction to hearing about their decision did not launch straight into banishment from the garden. Rather, he gave Adam a chance to take responsibility for his disobedience. It's as if God was saying, "I knew you would become conscious eventually. Now that you have, what are you going to do with this newfound realization? Will you choose to be informed by my spirit, or by your flesh?" As we'll see, this was also God's response to Cain when Cain's initial offering was not accepted by God.

For Adam, instead of taking personal responsibility, he decided to blame everyone else but himself. First his wife, then God. It seems to me that is where he missed the mark. Then Eve followed suit and blamed the serpent. Then everyone suffered.

I think God in the story wasn't expecting perfection, just honesty. (Creation was declared "good" not "perfect.") And when the humans decided not to be honest about their shortcomings, they were no longer permitted to remain in paradise.

Our willingness to bear responsibility for the pain from the first failure is where our power lies. We get to pick what to do with the pain. And maybe that's the same thing as finding our way back to the garden, the place where nature, culture, the individual, and families exist in harmony.

Sometimes we try to compensate for this first failure by trying to be perfect again and acting as if perfection is owed of us due to a first failure we experienced. But remember God's response. There is a space between the first and second failures. The first is going to happen, it just means we are humans that experience failure. Then

God's invitation is laced with language that says, "now that you don't have to be perfect, you can choose to be good" (to paraphrase John Steinbeck's line in *East of Eden*).

This same idea is repeated in the very next story with Cain and Abel. Right before Cain kills his brother and he is grumbling before God, God warns Cain that sin is a crouching creature waiting by the door, and it wants to devour him. But, God says, you still have a choice. Thou *mayest* conquer it. Its presence is inevitable. Its ruling over you is not.

**But the Hebrew word, the word *timshel*—
"Thou mayest"—that gives a choice.
It might be the most important word
in the world. That says the way is open. That
throws it right back on a man.
For if "Thou mayest"—it is also true
that "Thou mayest not."**
—John Steinbeck

Yet, it still seems as though acceptance isn't enough and that something must be done to correct such infinite wrongdoing. This deep-seated need is summed up by a British-American neurologist at NYU School of Medicine, Oliver Sacks, in his 1973 book *Awakenings*:

> *For all of us have a basic, intuitive feeling that once we
> were whole and well; at ease, at home in the world, totally
> united with the grounds of our being; and that then
> we lost this primal, happy, innocent state, and fell into*

our present sickness and suffering. We had something of
infinite beauty and preciousness – and we lost it; we spend
our lives searching for what we have lost; and one day,
perhaps, we will suddenly find it.

This is the psychologist's version of Genesis Chapter Three. To regain what we lost, we have to accept our responsibility for the first failure and allow forgiveness to do its work for the second.

So how can we ever have any hope of staving off the inevitably of failures and tragedies in our world? Can we ever find this thing we've lost?

Going back to Cain and Abel in Genesis Four, after Cain kills his brother, he cries out to Yahweh that his punishment of exile is more than he can bear. God does a curious thing by marking Cain in such a way that he would be left alone. It almost sounds like he gets off scot-free, but exile is no small punishment, and had the rest of the community had free license to punish the murderer, then the cycle of retribution would never come to an end. Humanity would be doomed from the get-go. As with the skins to cover Adam and Eve's nakedness, the mark for Cain, and later, the walled cities, was God's consolation to humanity which allowed them to still experience life after the fall.

Whether from the religious perspective or the psychological one, we all have an underlying sense that we live under a sort of curse where past traumas cannot simply be wiped away from our memories. We are cursed with enduring knowledge that our lives here are finite and that evil is a reality we must deal with. With this in mind, what can we do to blunt this curse? The cycle of revenge and vain, but primal, attempts at getting even has to be cut off somewhere or else revenge will always beget revenge; the Capulets and the Montagues would be locked in an eternal conflict, missing the point that the most important conflict to settle is within themselves.

But thinking back about the severity of what may have happened to us—or something we may have done ourselves—we might wonder how or why we would ever forgive such an egregious wrong. And, indeed, if you're in an actively abusive situation, the first priority may not be forgiveness, but safety. Ultimately, though, not forgiving someone means we become slaves to the wrongdoing, and instead of cultivating inner peace, we breed a life of bitterness. Holding a grudge is like lighting ourselves on fire hoping the offender dies of smoke inhalation.

Holding a grudge means we have not yet taken responsibility for our response to failure. It still remains someone else's responsibility to fix it and we become chained to whether the perpetrator ever truly apologizes or whether the justice system operates in a perfectly balanced manner—a curse in itself. The only way to undo this is through acceptance and forgiveness and once undone, far from letting the perpetrator off the hook, these activities are available to set *you* free.

The explanation of what forgiveness is and is not, is best summed up through an excerpt from Lewis B. Smedes *The Art of Forgiving*.

Things that forgiveness is not:

1. Ignoring or forgetting
2. Condoning or excusing
3. Tolerating or allowing further abuse
4. Reconciliation or restoration
5. Returning back to the way things were before
6. Allowing the offender to escape consequences

Now, what forgiveness is:

1. Giving up our right to retaliate or get even
2. Changing our heart toward the offender
3. Offering compassion instead of hatred
4. Unchaining ourselves from the person we blame; that which we blame, we give power to

Forgiveness is the only mechanism that allows humans to exist in harmony with one another, and how we can truly, finally, move on from the past. Forgiveness is voluntarily rendering up our right to get even, and in that exchange, we experience peace.

Forgiveness is not merely forgetting because it wasn't that big a deal. No, it's the opposite—it is necessary because the wrong was so real and such a big deal indeed. If the wrong is so real, then, like a kink in a piece of fabric, where exactly does that kink go? How can saying in our heart that we forgive someone undo that kink? In other words, how is redemption metaphysically possible?

In a legal sense, we might turn to some type of eye-for-eye system of retribution. But while the law code serves a role as a deterrent, it was never there to balance the cosmic scales. A wrong is a wrong, and just because a perpetrator is behind bars doesn't mean that sin has been atoned for. It might mean a human justice system has played its role in deterring reprehensible behavior, but it does not mean that a soul wound has been set right. Besides, we can probably think of many situations where the human justice system was not able to reach out and declare a just sentence on a wrong done. There are also things that are wrong morally that are not necessarily wrong legally, like cheating in a relationship. Even when the human justice system does pass a good sentence, a murderer might get 25 to life, but the loved one is still lost. Can life in prison fully reconcile the offense?

Ours is certainly not the first culture to navigate this challenge. Many before have always sought some sort of scapegoat, to take on itself the filth of our condition and to be exiled from the camp forever. The scapegoat enabled a just society because the wrong had somewhere to go.

In the Levitical law code, the instructions given to the priests were to literally lay their hands upon a goat, "confess over it all the iniquity of the people of Israel, and all their transgressions, all their sins, putting them on the head of the goat," and to eject the animal from their society. The goat in question had to be "without blemish." Blemished goats already have imperfections built in and cannot bear the imperfections of others. Scapegoating means to place onto something that is pure that which is impure, otherwise the filth of wrongdoing has nowhere to go and stays with the one who is at fault. This drive to cleanse by means of laying our mistakes onto something else which doesn't deserve it, and separating ourselves from that thing, has pervaded our culture for centuries. But does that work? Is this substitute hoofed animal actually doing anything in the metaphysical sense or is it a sort of outdated superstition? Maybe an economic illustration could help here.

There is debate among American politicians about the utility of what they call student loan "forgiveness." At first blush, that sounds like a great idea. Simply wave a government pen onto some paper and, poof, the debt goes away. But of course, the weight of the debt has to go someplace. This plan would be more accurately called student loan "transference," because it's not as if the balance can magically be set back to zero again. It needs somewhere to go because a charge has been placed and an outstanding balance still remains.

With money, it's easier to grasp the flow of that currency, but what about with debts that cannot be simply paid off with legal tender? That debt has to go somewhere. Setting things right metaphysically, or at the level of the soul, is only ever done with an act of forgiveness. And that act means nothing if there is not a universally accessible drain where all wrongs can somehow be made right again, where all the kinks can be buffed out, a cosmic scapegoat perfect enough that it actually has the load bearing capacity to remove the many stains of the world. The universal proclivity to sacrifice, to scapegoat, is rooted in this need to atone, to make right again, for the punishment for a wrong to go somewhere, to be borne somehow.

Perhaps, though, if forgiveness actually works as a remedy to soul wounds—and if we can take for granted that we need not operate on a paradigm of animal or human sacrifice as ancient religious traditions have done—then perhaps there is an alternative drain to all this wrongdoing that everyone has access to all the time.

I would offer that the answer to this is that such an alternative drain exists at the intersection of the world's place of greatest suffering, vulnerability, and humiliation—the high cost of absorbing all of humanity's failures. In a word, the Cross. It is the apex story of, by definition, the most unblemished lamb undergoing the most cruelty the world had to offer.

Why by definition?

Hero stories told over time are attempts at whittling down what the best story to tell about the human experience is. These narratives are attempting to answer the questions of what makes the best person, and in doing so, also provide a definition of what is the worst a person can be. The Cross is the place where those two things meet. Jesus was definitionally the best man—he was born of a virgin which means there was no sin passed down by the father (as the Hebrews conceived sin, it was always passed down by the father because Adam was the first to shirk responsibility), and every act he took, he did it for the good of others, all the way to the point of laying his own life down voluntarily. Recall the commonalities of heroes in Chapter Five.

He experienced the apex of suffering over the course of his story—multiple betrayals by close friends, abandonment by his culture, a sham trial, a forsakenness by his father, and essentially two torturous deaths (the flogging of 39 lashes was one short of what was considered fatal) at the hands of history's most infamous tyrannical ruler overseen by two approving governing bodies. This is the Messianic Archetype story, the ultimate story of healing.

Like in Harry Potter, an innocent child willingly lays down his life for his friends, allowing him to be reborn as a new creation that can at last take down the death eater himself.

When these apexes of innocence and sacrifice intersect, new life is created. When devouring trauma encounters a human willing to let go of their own understanding, new life can begin. Trauma gives us two lives; that's the paradox acceptance teaches us, that there is life after death, that a type of death can allow for the greatest life possible—not necessarily just life after our physical death, but new life today. This is how surrender (acceptance) can mean victory and how forgiveness can unchain us from a tragic past.

FUNCTIONS CHECK

1. Below are 10 modes of thinking that are the product of an incomplete acceptance journey. Thinking in this way leaves little room to hold two truths at once. Do any of these resonate with you?

   » *Being liked and loved.* I must always be loved and approved by the significant people in my life.

   » *Being competent.* I must always, in all situations, demonstrate competence, and I must be both talented and competent in some important area of life.

» *Having one's own way.* I must have my way, and my plans must always work out.

» *Being hurt.* People who do anything wrong, especially those who harm me, are evil and should be blamed and punished.

» *Being danger-free.* If anything, or any situation, is dangerous in any way, I must be anxious and upset about it. I should not have to face dangerous situations.

» *Being problem-less.* Things should not go wrong in life, and if by chance they do, there should be quick and easy solutions.

» *Being a victim.* Other people and outside forces are responsible for any misery I experience. No one should ever take advantage of me.

» *Avoiding.* It is easier to avoid facing life's difficulties than to develop self-discipline; making demands of myself should not be necessary.

» *Tyranny of the past.* What I did in the past, and especially what happened to me in the past, determines how I act and feel today.

» *Passivity.* I can be happy by being passive, by being uncommitted, and by just enjoying myself.

2. Journal exercise. What have you tried to "forgive-and-forget?" Is forgetting meant to be part of forgiveness? After reflecting on this section, can you answer the question, "who needs to be forgiven and for what precisely do they need to be forgiven for?"

GRATITUDE

The next evolution in post-traumatic growth is to practice being grateful for the life we've had, not despite, but because of the trauma we went through.

The most extreme, recent example in history of what this looks like can be seen in Aleksandr Solzhenitsyn's reflections on the Gulag—where tens of millions of people perished in the most unimaginable of conditions.

> *Bless you prison, bless you for being in my life. For there, lying upon the rotting prison straw, I came to realize that the object of life is not prosperity as we are made to believe, but the maturity of the human soul.*

So profound was his realization that life wasn't about material things, that he learned to be grateful for the source of all his harm. His greatest suffering was his greatest teacher, and so too it is for everyone, or at least it can be, if we have practiced accepting and forgiving.

Again, there is an important distinction here. This does not mean we go actively looking to lay in rotting prison straw or that we welcome the predations of an offender. Rather, it means that should such tragedies befall us, we see them as "first failures" that we can grow out of.

Inevitable tragedies of life make us more conscious of human nature, that we live not for material pleasures but for the maturity of the human soul. And this lesson is worth far more than any material wealth can offer us.

This is why we can practice being thankful for the worst seasons of our lives. Maybe we're not thankful for the evil lurking in a perpetrator's heart, but we can be thankful for what it is allowing us to become. A seed must be buried and broken open in order to fundamentally change into a tree.

Gratitude must also be a conscious practice because our threat detection systems cling to survival-based negativity far more readily than they cling to emotions of gratitude. In order for the emotional state of gratitude to do its work, we must actively hold on to that emotion for several seconds before it becomes wired into our brains, whereas fear responses wire far more quickly.

So, a gratitude practice might take the form of writing a few things down at the beginning of your day and right before you go to sleep, followed by a few moments of actively feeling the sensation of thanksgiving within yourself—or else the sensation might quickly evaporate as the Monkey Mind tries to take back over.

Be grateful in spite of your suffering.
—Jordan Peterson

FUNCTIONS CHECK
Stop reading now and write down three things for which you are grateful. Stay with the feeling and note where in your body that feeling arises. How does that affect your mood? If you were living a grateful life, what would an observer see you doing?

DIALOGUE
In various schools of psychology, the academics have attempted to create models of how the parts of the human mind can be categorized. For example, you may have learned about the id, ego, and superego in a psychology 101 class, and maybe you've come across

the idea of mind-body-spirit triad. We also briefly looked at the Internal Family Systems model in Chapter Three, another model useful in some cases.

Remember from Chapter Three that Internal Family Systems (IFS) offers a model using "parts" which is a term referring to a sub-personality. This theory operates along the assumption that each individual has multiple components within us that drive behavior. And if one of those parts is there to protect us, it can maladapt and offer this protection when it really isn't necessary.

Whichever model you subscribe to, one of the fundamentals of this idea is that when we have some type of malady or dysfunction, the parts are not speaking to one another properly. The parts are dis-integrated. In IFS, it's typically the "Exiles" who haven't come home to rest. Often, these Exiles are subpersonalities of a younger version of ourselves which are said to split from the central Self as a way to cope, but never came back home, a child needing loving care who never received it. Sometimes we must become our own mom or dad or even wife or husband, as strange as that sounds. Speaking with the parts allows them to reintegrate with the rest of the self, providing coherence between all the members. This is the same concept of integrating the archetypal wanderer previously discussed.

One other model that is a very approachable way of interacting with what often feel like very abstract ideas is the Positive Intelligence model. The "parts" of this model are composed of the "Sage Mind" and "The Judge." The Judge has a counsel composed of nine members that can turn to our internal saboteurs. There's the hyper-achieving saboteur, the victim saboteur, the controlling saboteur and six others. You can go online to positiveintelligence.com and take a test to see which of the Judge's saboteurs are in the driver's seat for you most of the time.

It can be extremely helpful to put names to those voices even if we can't necessarily scientifically demonstrate these parts; working on the model of "parts" is advantageous when it allows us to distinguish between something in us that is merely casting a vote, and the part of us which retains executive control. Without some sort of naming and categorization framework, those parts can feel like a very messy web of conflicting voices that can be extremely difficult to shut off.

This is, in part, the idea behind talk therapy. Simply by allowing the patient to think out loud, a healthy dialogue is created where the mind can begin to order itself. Our speech can subdue our otherwise sporadic parts and remind us who is in control and who needs to be put in their place. The exercise of free speech may be the cure, at least to some degree, of a disordered mind.

I say "to some degree" because the healing process needs to be nested with the other concepts in this chapter. Healthy internal dialogue is a necessary, but not sufficient, step to completing the hero's journey. I would offer that it's beneficial to everyone as at least a first step in organizing the mental clutter.

FEELINGS BEFORE YOU   FEELINGS AFTER YOU
TALK ABOUT THEM   TALK ABOUT THEM

There is a significant effort in the mainstream to destigmatize the realm of mental health. And it's great that therapy is becoming more normalized, especially for those who really benefit. But the admonishment to "just talk about it" to remove the stigma doesn't really work for all subcultures. In a culture that tends to scapegoat societal ills on an out-group, members of that so-called out-group end up not having a voice among the mainstream. No one is willing to listen, so what's the point of talking it out anyway?

I think the remedy here is to foster cultural change in that each member of society is seen to have equal value, or at the least, engender a sense of hope within the groups seeing the highest rates of suicide by cultivating change from the inside out. Veterans and white males specifically have some of the highest rates of suicide in America. How good are we doing at encouraging Veterans and middle-aged white men to live a purpose-driven life, injecting that subculture with hope that their stories, their lives, are not forgotten in our current cultural milieu of blame, victimhood, and cognitive decrepitude?

In the movie *Coco*, the main character gets a chance to visit his ancestors in the afterlife. What he discovers is that his ancestors only remained there so long as they were remembered on earth. As soon as the memory of someone's story was forgotten, they faded away forever.

Is that not how it works here and now? When an individual's story can't be told, and they cannot engage in a healthy dialogue, they begin to fade.

There is no greater agony than bearing an untold story inside you.
—*Maya Angelou*

If change is going to happen, it has to start at the individual level with close friends who are willing to lend a listening ear, because to tell one's story, someone else must be willing to receive it. Sometimes the "other" is just a blank page, and that's okay, too, but there will always be much more potency when there is an "other" with skin on to share the burden of agony, or in the joy of hope, discharged in the form of dialogue.

MEANINGFUL WORK

Speaking and writing one's story is the opposite side of the coin of acting out one's story. Storytelling and taking action based on one's story is how we make the narrative and the concrete reality coherent. We make these things fully realized when we engage in meaningful work.

Generally speaking, women are much better and have a more intrinsic sense about the utility of talking about their mental chatter in order to process it. Men, generally, can do this through an exercise of working with their hands. I don't think there is a absolute of how much of one or another is needed for healing, so, maybe one person would do well to spend just a little time processing through dialogue, and the majority of their time doing productive, meaningful work. Or vice versa.

Sometimes going out back to chop wood can be as therapeutic as free association (classic talk therapy on the sofa) with a psychoanalyst.

I think the kind of work we are after here is the kind of where where you can find yourself experiencing a flow state. Remember, flow happens when we're engaged in something highly meaningful to us. When it comes to meaningful work in this context, I'm not necessarily referring to that job you do eight hours a day, although it could be and I hope it is. This is the sort of work that you can do which doesn't drain you in an unsustainable, fatiguing way, work that you're competent at, and work that you find matches your skill level. Picture the guy in his garage working on his vintage Mustang without distractions, the teenage daughter practicing the violin in her room, the cyclist in the driveway taking apart the cassette to clean the gears.

When this type of work becomes your total vocation, this is known as *ikigai*, a Japanese term which describes the intersection of what you're good at, what you love, what the world needs, and what you can be paid for. We saw before that there is no single metric which shows clear-cut progress in a post-moral injury situation, but a "Post-Traumatic Growth Inventory (PTGI)" has been made that can offer some perspective on what we might look for in an individual on such a path. One of the five[8] dimensions of PTGI is "New Possibilities." Following moral injury, we must come to accept that many future possibilities we once thought were possible must be killed off. Orientation toward new possibilities makes sense as a marker of progression. If finding your own *ikigai* seems like an impossibility, ask yourself what story you're telling yourself about the future. We limit ourselves by internal monologues laced with "I should do this," "I ought to do that," "I can't take that risk." Thus our future possibilities are stuck in what we say to ourselves. Again, we can work to identify and update this way of thinking through all the tools in this chapter.

As we work to find our *ikigai*, we work to find flow along the way. Flow states are so important during and after processing through moral injury because this state is in many ways an exact opposite state of living out the story of unhealed trauma. Work and

---

8   The other four are development of more intimate relationships, greater sense of personal strength, greater spiritual development, and greater appreciation of life.

play which results in flow provides a marker that we have reached a balanced state of being, perfectly on the edge of enjoyment and challenge. Positive psychologist Mihaly Csikszentmihalyi, whose work did a lot to popularize this idea of flow state, said, "There's this focus that, once it becomes intense, leads to a sense of ecstasy, a sense of clarity: you know exactly what you want to do from one moment to the other; you get immediate feedback."

Contrast this state with the downward spiral of anxiety, isolation, and avoidance.

Tinkering, planting a garden, gaining competency on an instrument, doing fun work, these activities remind us that we still have a corner of this universe that is under our control, that a new possibility can be found in cultivating new competencies in activities we enjoy, and we can exert our abilities in service to something that is improving and making things better for everyone, even if we start very small. Even if it's as simple as five minutes twice a week participating in a creative human experience, finding this flow state can allow us to identify when we are on the right track because flow requires holding a tension, a paradox you might say, between optimal stress and optimal relaxation which results in creation. Moral injury and trauma recovery are not matters of eliminating stress to find peace; it's a process of properly ordering stress and rest in order to generate a brand new thing out of the Phoenix ashes of our old life.

So, where does the rubber meet the road when translating thoughts and stories into actions and work? In a word: participation. Spectators have no need for living by faith, for forgiving, for radical acceptance, for deep conversations. Spectators leach off of the shallow substance of substitutes and live shallow lives as a result. Participants act from faith that every part of their story matters, allowing them to experience the depth of all human experiences.

The participant is that man Theodore Roosevelt spoke of in his famous speech.

> *It is not the critic who counts; not the man who points out how the strong man stumbles, or where the doer of deeds could have done them better. The credit belongs to the man who is actually in the arena, whose face is marred by dust and sweat and blood; who strives valiantly; who errs, who comes short again and again, because there is no effort without error and shortcoming; but who does actually strive to do the deeds; who knows great enthusiasms, the great devotions; who spends himself in a worthy cause; who at the best knows in the end the triumph of high achievement, and who at the worst, if he fails, at least fails while daring greatly, so that his place shall never be with those cold and timid souls who neither know victory nor defeat.*

FUNCTIONS CHECK

1. Where have you seen the difference between the first failure and the second failure?
2. How can your first failure be transformed into a success? What do you need to take personal responsibility for in order to make that happen?
3. What do you consider a centering activity?
4. Was there an activity you used to love doing when you were younger that faded away in your adult life that needs revivifying?
5. What do you love to do? What does the world need? What can you get paid for? What are you good at?

CHAPTER 8

THE BIOLOGICAL SIDE OF TRAUMA

IN THE FIELD OF physical medicine, most conditions have well understood criteria for what constitutes a patient getting better. The bone fracture has been filled in, the tumor has shrunk, the coughing, sneezing, achy feelings are gone, and so on.

But when it comes to what we call "mental illness," the threshold between acute and well is blurry to say the least. For example, there is currently no industry standard for when a patient has been "cured" of PTSD, nor is there a consensus on what metrics to even use to measure what "better" is. It's not as simple as a temperature check because there exists no objective thermometer for the health of the soul. Some cultures don't even have a word for trauma which matches our meaning, thus their whole conception of where these thresholds of sick and well are is completely different. How do we know we've got it right? What's a good definition of "health?"

Is there something we can use instead? Most clinical trials that test PTS intervention strategies focus on symptomatology as it relates to the DSM-5 criteria we touched on in Chapter One. Those measures—like frequency of flashbacks, hypervigilant episodes, nightmares, etc.—have blurry lines. For example, say someone went from having two nightmares per week to reporting only one, but they're still experiencing just as much relationship turmoil and other problems in their life that haven't resolved. Or maybe someone is learning to be less hyper-stimulated in crowded spaces, but they are still only getting four hours of sleep a night. Are they getting better or playing whack-a-mole with the symptoms?

To illustrate the point, consider the list of other proposed markers of improvement for PTSD. These include levels of self-worth, social integration, aggressive behavior patterns, shame, emotional regulation, self-compassion, and even markers of chronic disease like Alzheimer's and Type 2 Diabetes, both of which are highly comorbid (occurs alongside) conditions with PTS. So, which is it? How do we know we're getting better?

In my late elementary years, I used to fish in a neighborhood pond a few miles from my home. The fishing there was usually good, but we had to be careful not to snag our hooks on an old, sunk picnic table. One day, I was fishing alongside a four-year-old and his dad. The young boy was slowly understanding how this whole fishing thing worked, and he was told that when the bobber goes underwater, it means you have a fish biting at the hook. Using this logic, he proceeded to crouch down on the pier and place his hand on top of the bobber, pushing it down, reckoning that that would mean there was a fish on the hook.

Sometimes, chasing symptoms of mental distress is a lot like catching fish by pushing the bobber under, focusing on above-the-surface patterns rather than asking deeper questions. The allopathic world of medicine has gotten very good at "pushing the bobber down" with various medications to make surface level pain go away, but if there is something wrong on the other end, it's only at best, half the equation.

The puzzle of discovering the best possible inputs and outputs of human mental and physical health is much more like a black box than a simple input-output machine. A black box model describes a system in which there are so many interacting variables between inputs and outputs that it's not possible to have a perfectly repeatable and predictable set of variables which always result in human health. Michael Pollan, in his *In Defense of Food* book, makes the case that nutritional science is continually confounded by our inability to draw one-for-one inferences based on inputs. He uses the illustration of the constituent chemical components of thyme. This plant has 38 unique, identifiable antioxidants which all have the potential to interact in the body in a different way. Food cannot be reducible to a few items on a nutrition label—isolated vitamins and minerals fail to have the same synergistic effect from a whole food source. This is to say nothing of the manifold metabolic pathways the body uses in response to its inputs that convert potential food energy into kinetic energy—a diagram of which would put to shame the New York City Subway map in its complexity.

On a model such as this, the best we can do is identify what generally works, what generally doesn't, and leave room for the black box complexity. How do you catch a fish? Generally, you go in the mornings and evenings. Generally, you hand-pick a lure for the type of fish you're after. Generally, there's a good cadence to reel that lure in to heighten your odds of a catch. But what about the pH of the water? What about the moods of the fish that day? What about the temperature fluctuations over the last week? What about the algae content? On and on. We can't know all the conditions because fishing is a black box activity. We have control of a few variables which usually enable anglers to catch fish, and we know strategies which definitely don't work. But we can never have a perfect cast which guarantees a catch. If we did, it would be called "catching," not "fishing."

Examining how capable the body is able to convert food energy into usable kinetic energy can reveal quite a lot about an individual's health, especially if they have a significant amount of concomitant mental distress. This is called **metabolic health.** A few markers relevant to metabolic health are fasting glucose levels, triglyceride to HDL cholesterol ratios, Interleukin-6, and c-reactive protein, the latter two being indicators of inflammation levels. No need to memorize these, but the point is that these objective metrics are already used to see which way the needle is moving on one's metabolic health. And if we can come to a better understanding of how the experience of chronic stress affects our ability to manage internal fuel stores, this can open the door to a whole new set of actionable strategies we can use to heal.

The mind and the body are so interwoven that acting on one will affect the other. The body is a projection of what is happening in the mind, and what's happening in the body also influences the state of the mind. We already explored how thoughts become signals to our cells, a mind-to-body influence on metabolic health. Here, we're looking at the other direction of influence. We may find that it can be much easier to turn the dials on our bodies to influence our minds to help us heal. And making changes in the body is much easier to track objectively than tracking psychological shifts. This is the main idea of this chapter: you can make a change to the body to change the mind. But we must respect that there is a black box component to this growth.

When the mind is experiencing chronic stress related to trauma, the body experiences inflammation. Inflammation is essentially the body's hormonal and chemical response to trauma, in all its various forms, within the body. It's an immune response to danger or to some sort of imbalance and too much of this response leads to disease. The inflammation process initiates healing after some event of adversity, like a cut, bruise, or sickness. If you have ever had gingivitis, you know what inflammation is like. The area is red, puffy, and highly sensitive to the touch. This is what inflammation is like in the rest of the body. Chronic inflammation brought about by poor diet and lifestyle factors shows up in the joints, gut, and blood-brain barrier. But not all inflammation harms our health.

Going to the gym and placing the body under a challenging load stimulates a degree of inflammation. This level of inflammation—done in sustainable doses—leads to growth. But many other things can cause the body to become inflamed as well—poor diet, a sedentary lifestyle, life-sucking relationships, and several other factors we will discuss.

So a little dose of stress leading to inflammation is good and helps the body process food energy into kinetic energy better, but too much will deteriorate us, having the reverse effect. So closely associated are poor markers of metabolic health and clinical PTSD that some researchers have even questioned whether PTSD is better thought of as a metabolic disease in disguise. By addressing metabolic health alone, one may gain a massive boost in their ability to grow from trauma. Of course it should be stated that insofar as psychological symptoms are affected by shifts in metabolic health, one's mileage may vary, but the reader has only something to gain by increasing their awareness of how movement, sun exposure, diet, and other lifestyle elements have direct impacts on their psychological well-being. It's already well-established, for example, that exercise has a far more powerful antidepressant effect, with none of the side effects, than prescription SSRI antidepressants.

Getting our metabolic health in order has much to do with modulating how inflamed we allow our bodies to get. The relationship between metabolic health and chronic inflammation is so strong that some evidence shows that individuals with higher rates of inflammation are more likely to develop PTSD following trauma exposure than those who are less inflamed *(all other factors being roughly equal)*. While the evidence isn't strong enough yet to demonstrate one-to-one causal factors, (that is to say, if you are 80% inflamed, you are twice as likely to develop PTSD—this level of causation has not been established) it still stands to reason that one's metabolic health is closely associated with the nature of one's experience with chronic stress following an intense moral injury.

Understanding the biological factors as they relate to trauma and healing can offer an easy onboarding ramp to improved mental health. In Chapter One, I introduced the idea that the psychiatric world may be relying more on hearsay than objective science to make clinical decisions regarding "PTSD" as they don't take into account the nature of the human soul. I also made the point that by putting a name to something, it gives us a better idea of what the nature of the condition is and thus, how to approach it.

While I was in ROTC, I was training at Ft. Benning late at night on a land nav course. I was paired up with another cadet, and we were waltzing along Main Supply Route Yankee after a successful night of finding navigation points, when, lo, a noise was heard just off the road in the bushes! It sounded much larger than a squirrel, and South Georgia is rife with all sorts of strange creatures that surely could tear us to pieces. My fellow cadet valiantly jumped behind me so the creature would get me first.

We cautiously made our way along the road until we'd put some distance between us and the multi-tentacled monster lurking in the bushes. Moments later, one of the cadres was cruising along the route doing safety checks in his pickup. We asked him whether he had seen ol' Monstro a couple hundred meters back.

"Oh, you mean that raccoon?"

Just by hearing the name of something, our relationship to it totally changed.

Various schools of thought in psychology will try and pin down the nature of the creature in the dark which causes our mental distress and what we can do about it. Maybe it's unresolved childhood trauma. Maybe the individual is blaming others too much. Maybe there are dysfunctional mental "programs" which replay old memories. And so forth. These are various forms of dragons, to borrow from the meaning of many Western mythologies.

To deal with these creatures, the clinicians will rely on "therapeutic factors" like cognitive restructuring, insights into the past, making "contact" with a past self or other family member, facilitating dialogue between parts, and so on. I'm not discounting any of that, and if you've read up to this point, I obviously place a decent amount of stock into those things, as many of them are fundamental to post-traumatic growth. It's necessary to visit the spiritual arsenal, outfitted with things like gratitude, acceptance, forgiveness, and hope, when dealing with dragons.

However, while all those therapeutic factors may help to resolve the very real dragon lurking deep in the forest, many of us would benefit from realizing the most pressing concern is the family of raccoons off the side of the road that must be dealt with first. This could establish a much needed beachhead on our journey toward post-traumatic growth. Indeed, in some cases, all there is are raccoons! Which is to say (and it should be stated, this is not medical advice), chronic inflammation may be *the* cause of one's depression or other mental distress, not merely *a* cause. Therefore, in many cases, treating our conditions as if they are this nebulous, mysterious entity that is passed down to us from the modern day gurus in the psychiatric world is not a good use of our energy. Maybe the bulk of our recovery and growth can simply be found in the process of chasing a new personal record for the back squat or deadlift, as everything that goes into chasing those records covers many bases in managing the physical symptoms of trauma.

I realize it's quite the claim to say that all a depressed person needs to do is change lifestyle factors that turn the dial on inflammation in order to get better, but there is ample evidence to suggest causal links between the two. At the end of the day, nearly 88% of Americans have poor metabolic health and are likely more inflamed than they need to be, so tackling inflammation is in everyone's best interest regardless of any mental health diagnosis.

The cascade of hormonal and chemical shifts that happen in the body and the precise mechanisms of how chronic stress relates to the body's ability to convert food energy into usable energy is beyond the scope of this chapter. But a simple way of thinking about it is how the body diverts its resources. Too many resources sent to the trauma-management department means that the digestion and recovery departments become starved and unable to function.

Most of the time, the body should not be upregulating its inflammatory pathways, but if the mind lives in a constant state of adverse thinking—hyper-vigilance, stress and ruminations about work, homelife, etc.—the body responds by constantly inflaming everything in response to psychological adversity.

Mental stress becomes physical stress. Physical stress stimulates inflammation. Too much inflammation for too long leads to diseases affecting our mental and physical well-being.

This state of too much inflammation for too long is called "chronic systemic inflammation" and has been identified, as mentioned before, as the primary root cause of modern diseases like Alzheimer's, Type II diabetes, cancer, and depression.

On the physiological level, chronic systemic inflammation is like calling up the National Guard to direct traffic in the everyday morning commute. A job they could do, but would be better used for other purposes. And if they do it all the time, it drains their ability to actually do the job they were primarily designed to do.

So why are so many people today chronically inflamed? The graphic below shows the sources of inflammation and sources of inputs that help regulate it.

INFLAMMATION LEVELS

INCREASED
- Industrial seed oils
- Sedentary living
- Social isolation
- Negative self talk
- Holding a grudge
- Wheat and sugar
- Processed foods
- Irregular sleep patterns

DECREASED
- Animal-based fats
- Regular, sustainable exercise
- Engaging with a social group
- Positive self talk
- Forgiveness
- Organic produce
- Routine wake times
- Sun exposure (before burning)

Basically, we're not consuming those things we were designed to consume or participating in lifestyle factors we were designed to participate in.

Consuming oils and wheat products not designed for our bodies, consuming unedifying speech, consuming modern comforts of the couch and easy media, and consuming constant stimulation through screens and late nights instead of good sleep—all of these in excess contribute to traumatizing the body all over again.

When we considered gratitude as an ingredient to post-traumatic growth, we looked at how the threat detection systems of the mind cling to dangers far more than they cling to positivity. Therefore, we have to actively remind ourselves of what is good and focus on that in a proactive manner. In a 21st century grocery store, we have to consciously apply effort to selecting the positive food sources as we do with consciously applying effort to practice gratitude.

Before the modern conveniences of grocery stores and innovations on the processed food front, most humans didn't have the option to pick a donut over a fruit salad. But now, about 70% of the food at grocery stores does **not** fall into the category of a "species appropriate diet" for humans. For example, the species of corn and wheat that are now so pervasive in our food system did not exist prior to about the 20th century. These foods are also major contributors to chronic systemic inflammation.

Seed oils, like vegetable, canola, sunflower seed, and cottonseed oil, cause trauma to our cells that the body responds to with inflammation, and most of our food today is drenched in them. Deep fried foods are completely soaked in these oils and the body must reroute immune system resources to deal with substances that we were never designed to eat.

We pay the price for eating these oils—found in high doses in virtually all fast food, many packaged foods, and in home cooked meals if that's what you're using—in the form of damage so harmful in the body it adversely affects DNA in a similar manner as radiation damage.

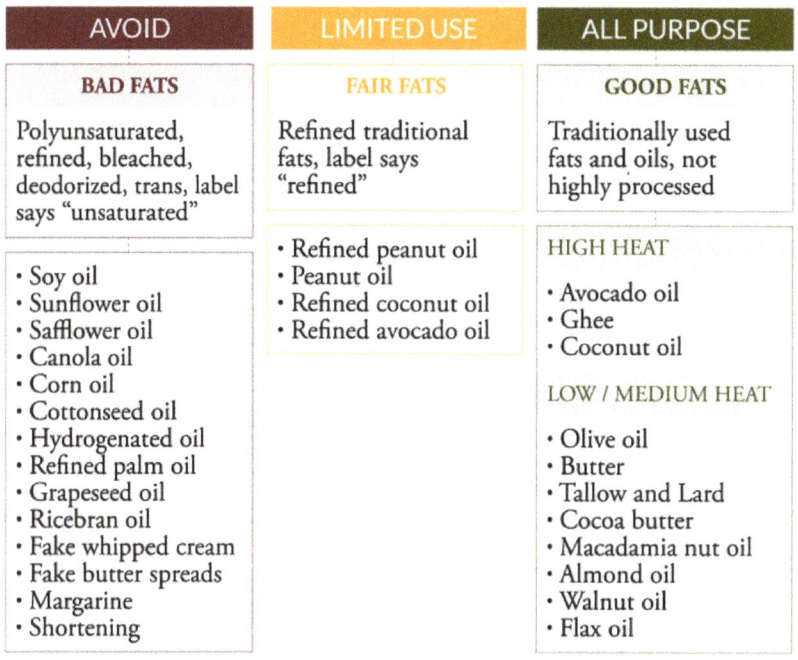

AVOID	LIMITED USE	ALL PURPOSE
BAD FATS	**FAIR FATS**	**GOOD FATS**
Polyunsaturated, refined, bleached, deodorized, trans, label says "unsaturated"	Refined traditional fats, label says "refined"	Traditionally used fats and oils, not highly processed
• Soy oil • Sunflower oil • Safflower oil • Canola oil • Corn oil • Cottonseed oil • Hydrogenated oil • Refined palm oil • Grapeseed oil • Ricebran oil • Fake whipped cream • Fake butter spreads • Margarine • Shortening	• Refined peanut oil • Peanut oil • Refined coconut oil • Refined avocado oil	HIGH HEAT • Avocado oil • Ghee • Coconut oil LOW / MEDIUM HEAT • Olive oil • Butter • Tallow and Lard • Cocoa butter • Macadamia nut oil • Almond oil • Walnut oil • Flax oil

When the body is fighting inflammation from unnecessary sources—that is, anything other than acute dangers or eustressors that are good in short doses, taking advantage of the body's anti-fragile nature—it's less able to respond to real toxins and other such damages.

TOO LITTLE STRESS	OPTIMUM STRESS	TOO MUCH STRESS	BURNOUT
DISTRESS	EUSTRESS	DISTRESS	DISTRESS
• No creativity • Boredom • Fatigue • Dissatisfaction	• Creativity • Progress • Motivation • Change • Incentive	• Anxiety • Panic • Anger • Exhaustion • Illness	

There is a veritable plethora of diet books written which I invite the reader to explore further on their own. But one primary thing to bear in mind is how the 21st century food industry has divorced flavor from caloric value. If what we consume is in any way hijacking our body's ability to properly detect what sorts of nutrition it should expect—by way of artificial flavors, sweeteners, fats, colors, and textures—then it's best to eliminate such options as much as is feasible.

A "species appropriate diet "for humans is pretty straightforward once we know what not to eat. Eliminating the bad could provide its very own powerful benefit before even beginning a discussion about the composition of the rest of the diet. What is left over when we subtract most modern grains (rice is the least objectionable), refined sugars, artificial fats, colors, and flavors? We have meat, fish, foul, eggs, nuts, seeds, fruits, and vegetables.

Purely pasture-raised animal products tend to be preferable to conventionally-raised products. Organic produce tends to be preferable to conventional. Foods that have traveled a shorter distance to reach the market tend to be preferable to those that have traveled a very long way. Wild-caught, sustainable seafood tends to be preferable to the farmed variety. Raw dairy tends to be preferable to pasteurized dairy for those who can handle the lactose. Saturated animal fats are perfectly healthy and should not be feared based on heart disease concerns, as such concerns have been roundly debunked.[9] Most Americans would probably do well to up their protein intake, other factors being equal. Animal protein tends to

---

9   Having said that, if you were to purchase meat that was raised on a Concentrated Animal Feed Operation (CAFO), that meat tends to accumulate more toxins given their poorer living conditions. These toxins tend to accumulate in the animal's fat stores. In that case, lean cuts should be preferred if you choose not to go the 100% Grass-fed, pasture-raised route.

be much better absorbed, gram for gram, than plant-based proteins. Organ meats should at least be considered as an addition to a few meals a week—for the meat eater—due to their high nutrient density. Collagen is an often forgotten addition to the diet and should be consumed in some form, whether via bone broth, eating meat off the bone itself, or from a marine-based collagen. Adding some source of fermented foods like kimchi, nato, or sauerkraut will tend to do good things to your digestion. Supplements which support magnesium, vitamin D, and omega-3 fatty acid are probably good for most people.

While there is plenty of latitude within these guidelines—and those with specific food intolerances should of course make adjustments—filling your pantry with at least 80% of these types of foods, replacing the aforementioned processed trauma food, will make a huge difference in your body's ability to handle stress. Of course, there is much debate as to where on the spectrum of nutrition one ought to land and an endless stack of studies supporting and debunking all sorts of approaches. So, here, just consider that it's likely that most of the benefit one realizes when shifting from a Standard American Diet to something with a higher nutritional bang for your buck, comes simply from reducing intake of fake oils, fake sweeteners, and highly processed grain products. Depending on your goals, the rest may just be details.

When the body is preoccupied with clearing out the toxins from the modern food system, the price is paid by our mood. Moods are less stable when we are chronically inflamed and far more stable when we eat a species-appropriate diet. This affects our relationships, our ability to focus on work, our sleep, and so much more. Maybe along with marriage or relationship counseling, we should consider skipping the drive-thru on the way home for the same reason!

ENDOCRINE DISRUPTING CHEMICALS (EDC'S)

An exterior threat to our physical health that is pretty new to our society are a class of chemicals referred to as EDC's along with exposure to radiation from sources our bodies never had to deal with before the modern era.

We hear a lot about so-called "harmful chemicals," and we may mentally categorize those into horrors like DDT, MSG, lead, or asbestos. And you may have heard the word "chemical" carelessly thrown around to make it sound like a health show host knows what they're talking about, how dangerous stuff is and what products you should buy. But just about everything is chemicals, so which ones are the harmful ones?

The big deal about EDC's is that they have the potential to prevent our body's chemical and electrical messaging systems from working the way they should.

One hormone in particular which is subject to the influence of EDC's is testosterone (T). There has been a dramatic decrease in T count over the last 50 years. While smoking, alcohol consumption, and a species inappropriate diet are all factors, one of the biggest factors is our exposure to plastics in our food and cosmetics.

Fertility rates have suffered as a result. Miscarriages and erectile dysfunction have been trending in a very concerning direction over that time period, too. In 2020, fertility hit a record low in the United States, and it's been declining in nearly every country.

Post-traumatic stress is also associated with impaired T functioning. This could be due to the high secretion of testosterone in a combat or high stress situation and the body's struggle to return to homeostasis long-term. One study found that male combat veterans had higher levels of T when checked at one and six months following deployment, and that the development of "PTSD" following the deployment was actually associated with T levels prior to deployment. In other words, poor pre-deployment testosterone health was predictive for PTSD post-deployment.

There is a particularly pernicious hormone disrupting chemical class that we are exposed to called "phthalates" (pronounced "thalates"). According to Dr. Shawna Swan, author of *Count Down*, one of the major explanations for all this hormonal decline is our exposure to phthalates in plastics. This ingredient makes plastics soft and flexible. Rubber tubing and even vinyl clothing have high levels of phthalates. Foods that pass through this tubing also have this problem. For example, milking machines use tubing lined with phthalates.

There is such a thing called "phthalate syndrome" which, along with fetal alcohol syndrome, is one of the few syndromes diagnosed at birth. Phthalate syndrome impairs reproductive organ development. The more phthalates the mother is exposed to, the greater the impairment in the reproductive system the child realizes.

Many cosmetics, scented air fresheners, and skin care products are high in phthalates. You can use the app Think Dirty to scan your products to see how many "dirty" ingredients are in it and to the best of your ability, scan those products prior to purchasing to decrease your exposure.

Another chemical all consumers ought to be aware of is called "glyphosate," also known as RoundUp. It is the most widely used pesticide in the world, yet its harm to human and animal health can hardly be overstated. A 2022 systematic review published in the International Journal of Molecular Sciences said of glyphosate:

It has been shown that exposure to this pesticide during the early stages of life can seriously affect normal cell development by deregulating some of the signaling pathways involved in this process, leading to alterations in differentiation, neuronal growth, and myelination (brain cell growth). Glyphosate also seems to exert a significant toxic effect on neurotransmission and to induce oxidative stress, neuroinflammation and mitochondrial dysfunction, processes that lead to neuronal death due to autophagy, necrosis, or apoptosis, as well as the appearance of behavioral and motor disorders…It is unequivocal that exposure to glyphosate produces important alterations in the structure and function of the nervous system of humans, rodents, fish, and invertebrates.

Depending on how much it's used around the home, replacing RoundUp with something like a non-toxic vinegar-based solution could be a very easy switch which could significantly affect the health of those living in the area.

Here are some more steps you can take to reduce your exposure to EDC's.

- Avoid conventional milk (it's been so pasteurized, most of the nutrition is shot anyway).
- Avoid processed beverages that have been pumped through rubber tubing—almost all store-bought juice, sodas, etc.
- Use BPA-free containers.
- Use glass, ceramic, and stainless-steel containers instead of plastic.
- Check the labels on body products using Think Dirty.
- Avoid soaps with synthetic fragrances. Essential oils as fragrances are preferred. If you can find tallow-based soaps at your farmers' market, those are great.
- If you eat the skin of a fruit or vegetable, buy organic. (For a detailed list of the most heavily sprayed produce, do an internet search for the annual "Dirty Dozen"). Otherwise, it's likely been sprayed with glyphosate.

- Limit the use of Teflon coated cookware. If used, keep on low to medium heat and don't ever scrape the bottom of the pan while cooking. Cast iron is a great choice.

- Avoid drinking from plastic bottles if you can. Especially avoid drinking from plastic bottles exposed to hot temperatures.

- Replace cheap salts with Redmond Real Salt or other salt that was not extracted from polluted sea waters.

- For skin and home care, If all else fails, use Dr. Bronner's 18-in-1 soap in place of most of your other cleaning products and you'll be good to go.

CHAPTER 9

___

SOUND BODY, SOUND MIND

HOMEOSTASIS DESCRIBES A STATE in which two opposing systems are in harmony with one another. If you have a reservoir of fresh water and a reservoir of very salty water, then put a permeable membrane between the two, eventually they will reach a balance where the saltiness of the water is uniform across both reservoirs. The only reason this wouldn't happen is if there were some other force preventing the salt concentrations from reaching this balance. Perhaps additional salt keeps getting added to one side, or perhaps the membrane is too fine a grid to allow the salt molecules across.

Nature does not like imbalances, whether salt concentrations, or, as we're observing here, hormonal imbalances.

Hormones are the body's messenger chemicals—how the cells send text messages to one another to react to the environment. This reaction is an effort by the body to return to homeostasis because some external stress has caused an imbalance.

We need to experience imbalances and work through the process of rebalancing ourselves in order to experience good health.

This may seem a little paradoxical. How can both of these things be true at once—our body desires balance, yet imbalances in the right dose are a good thing? This gets back to the idea of how we are antifragile creatures, where routine imbalancing actually improves our overall balance. We are not harmed by the exposure to low-level stressors, we are harmed by their absence. Small doses of somewhat predictable chaos enhance our ability to deal with much larger doses of less predictable chaos. Pursuing the horizon of homeostatic balance is the healthiest way to live.

One of the Four Noble Truths of Buddhism is that life is *dukkha*. Commonly translated as "suffering," *dukkha* may be better understood as "unsatisfactoriness." The idea is that there is constantly a sense in which we need to engage in a pursuit in order to be content with what already is. Paradoxically, we need to also learn to be content with what we have now to find peace. We must learn to hold the tension of being able to find balance with everything life gives us in the present, while not forgetting that there is a tomorrow which will require of us something that we did not bring to bear today. "I'm not where I want to be, and I'm not where I used to be."

A river stays the same by constantly changing—not changing so much that it either floods or dries up, but enough to sustain and grow life. It's a lot like swing dancing. When the lead and follower connect, the lead's hands are on the bottom and the follower's hands are on top. This is the starting position for a move called "the basic" and is where the pair starts all of their subsequent moves from. It is very often the case that for some moves, the lead's hand ends up on top of the follower's hand after a rotation. In that freeze frame, we'd say that's the "incorrect" hand position and the lead must initiate a follow-on move to "correct" it. But the movements of flowing into and out of "correct" and "incorrect" is the dance in itself. If the pair stayed in the "correct" position the whole time, they couldn't really initiate any movements. If they never "corrected," they'd have a hard time getting back into the "homeostatic" basic movement. The flow involved in the balancing act is the point, not staying in a kind of static freeze frame.

On the biological front, distress happens when too many of our messenger chemicals are produced, and the body becomes unresponsive to them. Like the boy crying wolf too many times, the body can become desensitized to stimuli. If we have PTS, that means the body is crying wolf in a sense and the signaling chemicals aren't "heard" as well by the body. To revisit the subject briefly, we might want to know why it is that the body would be designed from the outset in a way that would allow it to fall into such a state, reacting to something that's not really there in objective reality.

To understand the answer from an ancestral lens, consider the humble prairie dog. A prairie dog's defense strategy is to stay in groups and dig burrows that predators cannot access. The group is advantageous because a dozen pairs of prairie dog eyes are much better than one at spotting overhead predators. The alarm system is networked out around the burrows, so it only takes one member to spot the large talons for the whole town to be alerted. Now, these burrowing ground squirrels have almost nothing to offer in a head-to-head face off with a bird of prey or wild K9, so their alert systems must be highly attuned. Being caught in the crosshairs of Mr. Eagle or Mr. Coyote while out in the open offers little hope of staying off the dinner plate.

Therefore, the cost of responding to a false-positive—of sounding the alarm when there is no predator—is a drastically smaller cost than a false-negative—of not sounding the alarm when there is a predator. For survival's sake, the rodents would be better off erring on the side of alarm-sounding, even if that comes at the expense of running and hiding slightly more often than is truly necessary.

Applied to our experiences, we can get in a state of "burrowing" at the beckoning of an alarm system sending too many false-positives about the environment. Over time, this overly active alarm system can drain us of life force, as those chemical messaging systems are taxed again and again, keeping us out of homeostasis far too often. We need a way to recalibrate our systems such that we can respond appropriately to life's predators, while sparing resources that would otherwise have been diverted to responding to false-positives.

Physical exercise and focused breath work are two powerful tools to rebalance this sensitivity and ability to return to an optimal tension of stress and rest.

The body's stress response is switched on when we exercise, and it is also switched on by our thoughts about stressful things. Some activation, as we've seen, is good. The human body was designed to move in order to be healthy. There are many physiological systems which cannot even function without a baseline of moving around.

For example, the lymphatic drainage system is dependent on the muscles being used in a challenging way in order to process waste products. We are kind of like diesel-powered military vehicles which become far more susceptible to breaking down if they are never run.

Of course, too much stress response activation for too long makes it much harder to return to homeostasis. We only have a finite amount of stress energy to spend over our lifetimes, and an overactive stress response will deplete these reserves. However, exercise helps us practice getting stressed and then returning back to a calm state, increasing our ability to regulate the nozzle of stress response hormones. This can help us manage psychological stressors outside of dedicated workout time. By stressing the muscles in controlled amounts, we give our system a chance to experience the flow in and out of homeostasis, to experience what it feels like to get stressed and then to calm down afterward, instead of constantly being semi-stressed all day long, with little chance of returning to healthy baselines. Maintaining this balance is a continuous dance.

To have peace of mind, you have to have peace of body first.
—Naval Ravikant

When the major inputs of stress are chronically activated, we can fall into the distress zone. Chronic stress numbs the body to the biological signals that switch the stress response on and off. It's like if the thermostat in your home never gets the signal to stop pumping out heat once it's reached its preset temperature.

The hormone cortisol is a primary regulator of the stress response. After the stress response is initiated, cortisol plays the role of telling the thermostat to chill out. It's a feedback system—when cortisol begins to elevate, it tells the hypothalamus (the brain's equivalent of a thermostat) to stop releasing all the other stress hormones.

For those with abnormally *low* levels of baseline cortisol, there is an increased risk of developing PTS symptoms. The theory is that since the body is not sensitive to hearing the message of cortisol, then other stress hormones like norepinephrine and epinephrine are produced in too large an amount and act on the brain to "over-consolidate" memories, meaning that the memory hasn't been stripped of the original emotional charge it had when the event first occurred.

So does that mean that if one is dealing with chronic stress, one ought to increase cortisol production? By now, I'm hoping you're seeing a pattern. We must learn to stimulate and respond to just the right amount of cortisol that both prepares us for action, but doesn't deteriorate our systems long-term. Without conducting an experiment on each individual to monitor cortisol levels at regular intervals over the course of the day, it's hard to say with much precision whether someone is over-producing cortisol or whether someone is under-sensitive to it. Again, the idea is to participate in lifestyle practices which return us to a more Goldilox zone, the amount of cortisol that lands us in the "eustress" zone, neither above nor below. The theme is that by trusting the inputs talked about here, the outputs are better overall capability of growing from stress, whether we want to examine that hormonally, emotionally, or otherwise.

Healing the overactive mechanisms of the stress response means the body needs to become more sensitive to the shutdown signals. Again, exercise is a fantastic way to do this. You're giving yourself a small dose of stress—but not too much—so the body knows what to do with it. This chapter will provide a survey of what this will look like, and as with the section on diet, will not concern itself too much with the minutiae of a specific plan, just overall considerations of what to look for in a plan.

A good place to start with movement and exercise is to get at least 5500 steps per day, preferably outdoors, as this was about the minimum number of steps found in a study to decrease depressive symptoms.

Exercise is a far more potent antidepressant than any pharmaceutical available on the market. It's even more potent when done as a shared experience with others. Insofar as stress can be considered a chemical imbalance nothing works better than exercising and allowing the body to naturally restore its own balance given a healthy stimulus. Putting muscles under load opens up an internal pharmacy orders of magnitude more potent than anything in a pill. It's also important to incorporate both aerobic and anaerobic exercise (cardio and resistance training). Each type of exercise has a different positive effect on managing and getting rid of PTS and depressive symptoms.

While many exercise programs are often marketed as some kind of fancy, unique solution to producing washboard abs and all the rest of it, the best fitness routine is the one you can stick to. We all live in different bodies with different levels of absolute capability, so a robust workout strategy for the seasoned athlete will, of course, look very different for someone working to lose a hundred pounds. The message here is that getting in any kind of movement is still far better for your mind and body health compared to none. Still, it can be very helpful to find a well-established platform if you like to be coached, where you don't have to think too much about exercise programming.

If you want to find such a program, and one which has largely dispensed with the big box gym glamor, and that combines community, infinite variety, and accessibility to the widest audience, I would offer that the CrossFit model is about the best on the market.

One thing that sets CrossFit apart from your average boot camp or spin class is that their model states in plain language exactly what they mean by "health" and "fitness" and how their workouts maximally contribute to both of those things. In short, "fitness" is defined as the ability to produce measurable work output across a variety of time domains and physical functions; health takes the same definition and applies it across a lifetime, i.e. how well can you continue to produce this work output across a lifetime. It was originally designed to combat modern diseases like Type 2 Diabetes, which as we know, commonly occurs with PTS, (and improving classic PTSD makers are associated with improving markers of Type 2) and to be scaled to allow the greatest number of people and their backgrounds to fit in—not necessarily to create Olympic-level CrossFit Games athletes and unwarranted ridicule from Chiropractors. Rates of injuries among CrossFit athletes are not significantly different from other sports.

It's always important to consider who your coach is and what your opportunities and limitations are when beginning any new exercise program. But aim to include lots of movement throughout the day (5500+ steps), 2-3 sessions of aerobic exercise per week (this is work done at or below a threshold heart rate of 180 minus your age, or conducted at an effort where you can hold a conversation), 2-3 resistance training sessions (which can include body weight), and sprinting once every 10 days or so with lots of recovering in between. These sprint sessions might look something like 5 rounds of 10 seconds sprinting full-gas (this could be running, stationary biking, rowing, etc.) with 2-3 minutes in between bouts. I would recommend looking into the Primal Blueprint model for elaboration on these guidelines.

There are plenty of other ways to train to glean the manifold benefits of both increased cardiovascular and muscular strength, but if you're not really sure where to get started, following a three day on, one day off routine doing CrossFit will get you 90% of the way there. An honorable mention should also be given here to the growing popularity of rucking. To ruck, all you need is a backpack with some weight.

Michael Easter makes the case in his book, *The Comfort Crisis*, that carrying heavy loads over a long distance through the wilderness is the original, optimal human workout. How else would we have transported our kill or gathered supplies back to camp? Rucking has a lot of advantages over other forms of training. It's very easy to incorporate into routine walks you might do with your family, you can increase the difficulty for yourself while walking the same speed as those around you, it combines elements of strength and endurance training, it has a low cost of entry, and there are many groups forming now that go on group rucks, so there is a strong social component. (Check out goruckevents.com for events in your area).

Aim to build up to carrying about 30% of your body weight for up to an hour and a half at a time. If your posture is something you're working on correcting, it is advisable not to use a weighted vest which places equal load around your chest as on your back. When the load is properly situated on your back, this can have a posture-corrective effect.

I should emphasize here again that for someone who isn't doing much exercise at all, just about anything that raises your energy output above baseline is going to have dramatic benefits if done consistently. When starting a routine, it can be tempting to fall into an all-or-nothing mindset. "If I don't go every day, I might as well just not go." I would encourage such a reader that taking any step toward moving more has benefit in and of itself, even if only a 5 or 10 minute walk. It's also worth emphasizing that including regular movement throughout the day is just about as important as that one hour trip to the gym or trail run. The body does not respond well to staying still for prolonged periods, even if, and per-haps especially if, you challenged your muscles earlier in the day. In fact, there is such a thing called "Active Couch Potato Syndrome" which is just what it sounds like. It describes someone who might get their hour of training in during the day, but the rest of the time is spent driving a car, sitting at a desk, sitting in front of the TV, sleeping, or otherwise not doing much moving. It turns out, one hour of movement in a day isn't going to offset the 23 sedentary hours of the day.

Genetics and your personal interests can also play a big role in what type of exercise is the best fit. I'm the type of athlete that has to do a ton of work to put on any muscle at all, however, I can make rapid adaptations that lend themselves to endurance performance. I confirmed this with a genetic test through DNAfit and indeed, I was heavily skewed toward endurance development. However, I was by no means confined to a single sport or type of exercise if I wanted to stay fit.

For many years, I followed the Primal Endurance model—as described in the book of the same name—as I was more interested in swimming, biking, and primarily running. Over the years, I've settled into a hybrid of the two with a CrossFit endurance model—which you can read more about in Brian MacKenzie's *Unbreakable Runner*. It's allowed me to enjoy a plethora of sports and see progress in everything from the clean and jerk to cross country skate skiing. That's what seems to work for me. I just say that to illustrate that with these guides, there is a tremendous amount of latitude someone can have in selecting a movement routine that's fun, dynamic, and, most importantly, sustainable.

BREATH

Breathing is the anchor for every system in our bodies.

Generally, the fewer breaths you take per minute at rest, the more efficient your body is at using that air to produce energy. If you are taking more than about 12-14 breaths per minute, it could be an indication that you have much to gain from learning to breathe better. For individuals with asthma or some type of panic disorder, they may be breathing as often as 20 times per minute. That is not enough time for the lungs to fully expand and to receive a full breath. Interventions that simply help the patient slow down their breathing can have significant effects on their symptoms, improving mood, cortisol response to stress, and attention span.

The word for the primary muscle involved in filling and emptying the lungs—the diaphragm—means "a fence between two things." As we learned, the breath is a curious and unique function because it can both operate independently of conscious thought and can be harnessed on the fly. The breath is the fence between the conscious and unconscious mind. It affects the operating status of every other system in the body.

Deep breathing brings deep thinking and shallow breathing brings shallow thinking.
—Elsie Lincoln Benedict

To look further under the hood, the lungs have receptors for activating both the stress response and the calming response. The stress response receptors are at the top of the lungs while the calming receptors are at the bottom of the lungs. The pattern of breathing we use can actuate the release (or not) of various arousal signals. When we take shallow breaths, we activate stress responses. However, when taking deep breaths, especially when including slow exhales, we will have the opposite effect.

So, if we're breathing very shallow breaths, we are not sending the signal to the body to be calm, as the breath is not reaching those off switches located at the bottom of the lungs. However, if we can learn to fully engage the diaphragm with each breath, our bodies can't help but relax.

In any good marksmanship class, the coach will teach the student to time their shots with their breath. The best pattern of breathing for shooting is a slowed, controlled breath with about equal time on the inhales and exhales. The most accurate shots tend to be taken at the bottom of an exhale where the diaphragm is relaxed, yet active. This is the challenge of the biathlon where cross-country skiers must transition from racing on the trails to calming their hearts enough to take aim at their shots. The task is to perfectly balance stress and relaxation. When the inhalations and exhalations are performed on the same interval, say, five seconds in, five seconds out, the body is receiving a signal to put the fight-or-flight and rest-and-digest aspects of the nervous system into a level see-saw balance. This breathing pattern is known as coherence breathing, as it creates a harmony between excitement and calm, facilitating states of flow.

We can easily take our breathing patterns for granted, reckoning that it's just a basic task of the human body, that we don't need to worry about learning how to do it. However, in another example of evolutionary mismatch, our modern world has not lent itself to allowing its human inhabitants to breathe correctly. Why might this be? Part of it has to do with inadequate nutrition which impairs the facial muscles and bones from growing into shapes conducive to a broad jaw, which lends itself to fitting even the wisdom teeth in place.

Isn't it weird that so many people today get their wisdom teeth removed because their jawline doesn't have room for it? What on earth did we do before? Did we have to find an ice skate and a rock to manually remove teeth from our jaw, a la Tom Hanks in *Cast Away*, all that time? Or did something change?

In the early 20th century, Dr. Weston Price, a Cleveland dentist, was compelled to find out what was different about Western jaws and face structure compared to people living in accord with their ancestral ways. He traveled the globe and found that peoples who adhere to their traditional diets almost without exception, had very broad facial structures and experienced no sort of tooth decay like his patients back in Ohio had. Their diets contained about four times as much calcium and ten times as much fat-soluble vitamins from animal foods than the average American.

So diet, face structure, and airway development clearly go together. But another feature of these peoples was their ability to breathe through their noses with much greater regularity than Western peoples, even when running and playing sports. Why does that matter? With every breath you take through the mouth, there is no barrier between air on the outside and the air that hits your lungs. Breathing through the nose conditions outside air before it goes into your lungs, changing it to a more optimal tempera-ture and humidity, while filtering out all sorts of dust and molds. So dramatic is the difference between the quality of air taken in through the nose and that of the mouth, that it's been found that even cognitive abilities are affected by students who were primarily mouth breathers versus those who were not.

Nasal breathing also affects the shape of the face. Try this. As you're reading this, with your mouth closed and your breath com-ing in through your nose, what is your tongue doing? Is it laying flat across the bottom of your mouth or pressed against its roof?

The upward pressure of the tongue on the face is necessary for proper face development. In the animal kingdom, very few crea-tures mouth breath unless they are sick, with the obvious exception of panting dogs staying cool. The nose is for breathing and the mouth is for eating. Without good tongue posture, the lower por-tion of the face tends to jut forward, causing impairments to our ability to take a good breath.

Controlling one's breath is often a technique recommended by therapists to control stress responses. Sometimes, this can seem like throw away advice because it seems like a trivial technique in light of what might be some serious mental distress. However, pairing breathwork with some of the other practices in this book has incredible potential to round out a return to a healthy human state. It's difficult to understand the profound impacts the breath has on long-term health and on stress recovery. When we practice taking conscious control of our breath to change our physiological state, paired with aerobic-boosting exercise, we can train ourselves to breath less, thus more efficiently.

To practice breathing better, one of my new favorite apps is called State. It is a highly simplified, super minimal, breath guide which learns your breathing patterns as you provide it input. It has quick options for being present, focused, needing to sleep, and needing to calm down.

There are a myriad of breathing techniques one can find with a simple internet search, so the methods below are certainly not an exhaustive list. The books, James Nester's *Breath*, Patrick McKeown's *The Oxygen Advantage*, and Wim Hof's, *The Wim Hof Method*, are replete with guides on breathwork.

Box Breathing

A quick YouTube search for "Box Breathing" will yield many videos that can guide you through the technique. This method gives a better overall balance within your nervous system, a harmony between alertness and calmness. The pattern is 5-5-5-5, as in 5 counts for an inhale, 5 counts for a hold, 5 counts for an exhale, 5 counts hold, and repeat. Use this technique ahead of focused work.

Mewing

Mewing, named after Dr. John Mew, is an exercise for the tongue and jaw, which, when done enough, can influence facial shape and potentially help with preventing crooked teeth. One of the consequences of introducing so much processed food in our diet is that it reduced the amount of effort needed by our jaw to eat. If all we had to eat was unprocessed, lightly cooked meats and plant matter, our jaws would have had much more use than they do today. Now, though, a lot of our food is soft, reducing the need to chew. Mewing is a technique to correct this mismatch.

To Mew, you want to make a sort of vacuum between your tongue and the roof of your mouth by engaging the back third of the tongue. Sit up straight as you do this. Draw down your tongue as you draw your neck straight. Think about almost swallowing your tongue while keeping it pressed to the top of your mouth. Keep your teeth together and lips closed. This will sort of be the posture of the tongue when you make an "ng" sound, as in "sing."

Consider incorporating this while sitting at a red light or while watching TV.

The 4-7-8 Technique

Exhalations switch on the calming response while inhalations switch on the stressing response. A breathing technique that emphasizes the calming response is the 4-7-8 technique. Inhale for 4 counts, hold for 7, and exhale for 8 counts—twice the duration it took to inhale. Repeat 10-12 times. Use when you have a few moments to yourself and need to calm down, or ahead of going to bed.

Physiological Sighs

Have you ever noticed that when someone cries, they tend to adopt a certain breathing pattern? It's something like two quick inhales and a release. This, in fact, is a breathing technique known to return the body back to a state of calm. It can also occur spontaneously when one is in a claustrophobic environment or during sleep when too much CO_2 has built up in the blood. You don't need to wait until the next showing of a sad movie to practice this technique. You can do it any time you're feeling anxious, and it only requires 1-3 rounds.

To perform a physiological sigh, take a big inhale through the nose, then inhale again (a double inhale) as much as you can, then exhale slowly through the mouth, allowing the shoulders to gently slide down your sides. If for some reason you cannot use the nose and mouth in that way, use whatever airway is available with the same pattern.

Use these during acute states of stress when you need to rapidly return to baseline. This might be incorporated when implementing the first step of the OODA loop discussed in Chapter Seven.

ADVANCED TECHNIQUE: WIM HOF

This technique is named after the man who brought it into popularity. The technique has allowed his body to withstand extreme cold and has allowed him to be able to consciously control his immune system after many years of practice.

It charges up the body, changing the pH in the blood, temporarily activating the stress response, and teaches the body how to calm down that response in controlled doses. I mentioned that exercise is a good way to let the body engage in a refractory period where the stress hormones are brought back into balance. The Wim Hof technique largely does the same thing, but through breathing.

The basic technique is as follows and consists of 3 to 4 rounds:

One round = 30-40 quick breaths, "fully in, letting go," which can be through the mouth. (This mimics what the body does when exposed to rapid cold.) Then on the last breath, exhale fully and hold for as long as you can. You may begin to feel a tingling sensation. Then breathe in and hold for 15 seconds. Exhale fully, then go straight into the next round for at least 3 rounds. Make sure you're doing this while sitting or lying in a safe area.

That's it.

It may be beneficial to do an online search for an instructional video. Enter "wim hof breathing follow along" and you should find what you're looking for. As you get more used to the breathing technique, you can practice with longer rounds. Personally, I feel a massive difference when I do three rounds of three minutes of breathing—so 70-90 breaths instead of 30-40. I learned the 3 minute round technique when participating in a local group breathwork practice, which you might consider looking into if that's available.

Visitors to Wim Hof's camp have been able to dramatically increase their cold tolerance with just two weeks of practice. There's a lot of promise with this technique and others like it to allow individuals to gain more conscious control of their stress response.

Our breathing has the ability to enlighten and activate any physiological mechanism in conscious control.
—Wim Hof

FUNCTIONS CHECK

1. Develop a sustainable workout plan which includes some aerobic exercise and some resistance exercise.
2. Practice one of the breathing techniques above for 5-10 minutes sometime today.
3. Following a bout of exercise, immediately incorporate box breathing to give your body a double dose of hormonal balancing practice.

CHAPTER 10

TIME OUT

WHILE BREATH WORK AND exercise are energy-expending efforts that help teach the body to return to an even keel after a stress, here we will examine the other side of the coin. One of the lessons I learned when training competitively for triathlon is that rest days required energy expenditure as well. Sometimes, the hard charging type-A gets a great sense of accomplishment by grinding, chopping, and producing results in a tangible way. They (speaking as one who tends to fall into this category) wear their accomplishments with pride and may fall prey to the temptation of forming their identity around what they have done. It sounds impressive to maintain a super disciplined routine of waking early, working out often, producing record sales and so on. But for this person, taking a break and allowing the body to do all the work to repair...that's the actual challenge. Grinding, to a point, can distract us from addressing our deeper need for restoration.

Many religious traditions have a ritual time out on a daily, weekly, and annual basis. The Hebrew word for the weekly time out is *sabbat*, the root of the word sabbatical, or an extended time away. This word simply means "to cease." To stop one's regularly scheduled program to allow for time to recompose and refresh.

The body doesn't know when to quit; it is very bad at saying "no" to things. The ego can have this tendency to think that, like a shark, it needs to constantly be on the move to stay alive. And of course, there's nothing wrong with that drive in itself. However, there is a time for everything, a time for chopping the tree and a time to sharpen the ax. Taking time to cease our work daily, weekly, and annually is good both for keeping our egos under control and for allowing our bodies to repair such that when we do get back to work, we may find we end up being more productive over the course of the year than if we just white knuckle our way through. Which brings us to our first strategy to *sabbat:* sleep.

While the cultural conversation around sleep is starting to shift, there is still a rather pervasive notion that sleep is mostly an inconvenient gap between waking hours. This is evidenced by the current state of sleep in the country. Forty percent of all American adults are sleep deprived. Poor sleep contributes to chronic inflammation and is associated with increased risk of cardiovascular disease. You'll almost never find someone with an acute psychiatric illness who doesn't also have a significant impairment in their sleep patterns.

The truth is that without sleep, we cannot heal. The body "at rest" is really not at rest at all, depending on which physiological systems you're looking at, and is hard at work consolidating everything that happened over the course of the day. Some parts of the brain are even far more active asleep than awake. The recovery process itself takes energy—it's far from a time period of stasis. Repair, reproduction, locomotion, and growth all draw from the same reservoir of available energy which means sleep in one sense restores energy, but it takes energy to do so. In order to reproduce and move, we must also have dedicated periods of repairing and growing.

A full night's rest which allows time for both mind and body recovery refreshes the part of the brain in charge of personality expression, executive planning, rationalizing, and many of the other behaviors which make us human. Poor sleep slows neurotransmission in this part of the brain, and the best we can do, when lacking sleep long enough, is behave in a more survival-based pattern. When we are sleep deprived, we are much more likely to see the world through a negative lens, and research shows that less sleep is very closely associated with getting into more arguments at home.

The body tends to prioritize its physical healing ahead of mental healing because if it had to choose in an extreme situation, it would make sense that the body needs repair first; it doesn't take much executive function to fight or run. Thus, if we cannot process through the full cycles of sleep, we cannot experience the mental first aid which later stages of sleep, occurring after around three or four hours, provide.

Our creativity, our ability to see problems in a new way, tanks when the mind has not been given sufficient rest. An element of post-traumatic growth is seeing new possibilities with our lives, and when sleep is impaired, our brain's ability to do so is impaired in kind.

As much as the ego may protest, there is no substitution for good sleep. Across the 20th century, militaries have been trying to come up with ways to stimulate their troops for long-term warfare. They came up with various classes of amphetamine drugs to make it happen. The Air Force tried, with the financial backing of the US Government, to come up with alternate solutions for sleep for their pilots. Nothing worked. You simply cannot win this fight against biology.

Yet, actually achieving a good night's sleep seems nearly impossible for many living in the modernized world. And especially for an individual with PTS, poor sleep prevents the brain from properly consolidating memories, stripping them from their emotional charge. It can turn into a vicious cycle of negative feedback. I can't sleep because I have intense negative emotions at night because I can't sleep. On and on.

While there could be some significant psychotherapy needed for an individual with intense and vivid nightmares and severe insomnia, here, we will go over non-clinical strategies to stack the deck in the favor of the body's healing. It may be that one of the primary "raccoons" when it comes to sleeping and healing falls within these principles.

To allow ourselves to sleep, we need to optimize for several factors which our ancestors living in a pre-modern world mostly didn't have to concern themselves with: temperature, light, schedule, and safety.

The first public displays of mechanical clocks in the West could be found in England in the year 1288. Prior to the widespread use of clocks, the sun kept the time. Our sleeping and waking hours would be much more in accord with the Earth's relationship to the sun, not in relation to our invented system of timekeeping. And this is to say nothing of the absurd notion of changing our clocks forward and back an hour twice a year. For most of history, our bodies only received cues from natural light which heavily influenced our circadian rhythm, the routine ups and downs of excitatory and calming hormonal signals we experience each day. With only rudimentary insulation, night time temperatures would have been much lower than most of our climate-controlled homes now.

Today, we are faced with the task of mimicking this sleep environment but with the added obstacle of 21st century luxuries such as cushioned beds, fiberglass insulation, and artificial sources of light available at all hours. This is a very similar challenge to many of the other lifestyle factors we've looked at in this book, and like those, the proposal is rarely to go back and make our life experiences just like it used to be before our current standards of living. Rather, it's a process of augmenting. We want to make our sleep environment in the home replicate a sleep environment while camping, just without the bears and extreme cold weather.[10]

One of the first things you might consider when refining your sleep is your sleep schedule. Maintaining as regular a bedtime and wake time as possible is ideal, especially your wake time. It can be tempting to adjust schedules over the weekends, but we've all experienced the dread of a groggy Monday morning that followed a weekend of late nights and late mornings. Maintaining a predictable sleep and wake schedule makes it easier for our resting bodies to take advantage of the timed release of hormones throughout the day.

In the morning, it's normal to get a shot of cortisol to jumpstart the system. This first jumpstart cues a day-long cascade of timed hormone release until melatonin, a primary driver that makes us feel sleepy, is at last released in a larger dose after the sun starts to set. Light exposure, especially via the eyes, is the primary cue for this hormonal harmony. We need to expose our eyeballs to the right doses of sunlight at the right time of day to get our hormonal rhythms in balance. Practically speaking, this would look like getting into natural light shortly after waking and reducing artificial light exposure starting around two hours before sunset.

Disruptions to this circadian cycle come in the form of blue light exposure too late in the day—which suppresses melatonin release—alcohol consumption, noise and novelty exposure, sleeping in too hot of a bed, and eating too soon before bed.

---

10 Longevity expert, Dr. Peter Attia, has even taken to camping out in his back yard as he found he consistently got better sleep by sacking out each night on a one-hundred-dollar air pad instead of a luxury memory foam mattress.

Blue light refers to a specific wavelength of light which uniquely signals receptors in the eyes to stay awake, that the sun is still high in the sky. Light emitted from fires doesn't contain this wavelength in enough of a dose to have this effect. In fact, it's much the opposite; watching a campfire before bed can aid the body in flowing seamlessly through the sleep cycle. Blue light blocking glasses have become more popular as this research has, excuse the pun, brought this phenomena to light. While it's best to avoid too much artificial light exposure altogether after the sun sets (our skin has photoreceptors as well which influence circadian rhythm), if we do choose to look at a screen for a work task or entertainment, a good pair of these might be the next best option.

Alcohol is considered by many to be a sleep aid, and while it can certainly help one transition from consciousness to unconsciousness, that doesn't equate to good sleep. Alcohol is a sedation aid, not a sleep aid; they are not the same thing. Even a single glass of wine is enough to disrupt sleep cycles and cause wakefulness throughout the night, even if we don't remember waking up. Alcohol also gets in the way of growth hormone release during the night, inhibiting our ability to fully repair physically by the next morning. So, we might have our reasons for finishing the day with a glass of adult beverage, but let's not kid ourselves into thinking it is for helping us sleep—and remember that the health benefits from the wine are from the grapes, not the alcohol.

Another issue with alcohol is that it places a high demand on the liver and while that organ is dealing with the toxin, it heats up. This can further impair sleep because the body needs to cool in order to sleep well. Our bodies are coolest sometime around two in the morning and begins this dip in temperature around the time we go to bed. We can enhance this process by taking a hot shower or by using a sauna about an hour before bed. While this might seem counter intuitive, the body has a cooling mechanism which you can trigger by making yourself hotter, then cooling off at a more rapid rate. You could also use a smart thermostat which decreases the home temperature starting an hour or two before bed, staying cool throughout the night, then gently rising as the sun comes up. Some innovative companies have also started developing bed liners which cool the sleeper from under the fitted sheet, aiding the body all night long to maintain a good sleeping temperature. A bonus to that solution is that if you sleep with someone else who has a different preference for temperature, you can make that adjustment for just one side of the bed. A cheaper solution would be to try wearing socks to sleep, which can draw heat away from your core and into your extremities.

Cooling the mind of racing thoughts can present a more difficult challenge than cooling the body with a shower or cold pad under the bed. There is a time in the day for problem solving, but right before bed is not it. To cool the mind, the first and easiest change to make is to place your phone out of view, preferably out of the bedroom entirely. The mind loves novelty because novelty has the potential to show us new ways of solving problems. Modern phones are novelty-producing machines, but most of it is the processed food equivalent of content. But the brain gets a similar hit of pleasure from that red circle notification as it does from that ripe red berry in the bush. Just by its presence, the mind almost can't help but think about what sort of novelty there is to find on that magic rectangle. Consider putting your phone into grayscale mode to reduce the novelty signals it sends to your brain and leave it charging in another room overnight.

"But my phone is my alarm clock," I hear you thinking.

It might be time to reframe how you wake up as well. We sleep in roughly 90-minute cycles, the time it takes to progress through the various phases of deep, light, and rapid-eye movement sleep. There is a way to align your wake time with the tail end of one of these cycles where you're already closer to wakefulness. If you've ever woken up in the morning feeling particularly groggy even though you'd been asleep for quite some time, it could be that you woke up at the bottom of a sleep cycle instead of at the top. Hitting that snooze button and going right back to sleep restarts the same problem; snoozing keeps your body in this groggy cycle of falling back into deep sleep then being jolted back into a wakeful state. Most of the time, you'd be better off waking up maybe 20-40 minutes earlier at the top of a sleep cycle than 10 minutes later at the bottom.

How can we time this better? Well, first off, consider how alarming a loud noise is first thing in the morning. Who in their right mind would want the very first noise they hear in the day to send an obnoxious sound of stress straight to the brainstem? I'm sure many of us still know the exact noise beckoning them to get out of bed to get ready for middle school, that god-awful buzz. Instead, how about an alarm clock that mimics the sunrise and gives the sleeper a half hour window to awake naturally? So, say you want to get out of bed by 6:00. A sunrise alarm clock will start lighting up using a half hour dimmer function, starting at 5:30, gradually increasing the intensity of the light. Then at 6:00, will start playing bird sounds when it's at peak brightness. Far more civilized. Of course, the exact function may change depending on the model, but that's the idea.

Another basic strategy would be to finish your last meal of the day about two hours prior to bedtime. When building habits, it's very useful to have an anchor activity from which other habits can sort of cluster around. A night time routine might start by putting dishes away, then after that, you might start practicing a flow of activities that are about the same each night. The brain loves regularity, and by participating in a fairly set schedule of tasks an hour or two before bed, we can begin to train the brain with activity cues which can help to send that signal to release sleeptime hormones.

SAFETY

An aspect of a good night's rest that can be taken for granted is our sense of safety in our space. It shouldn't need much explanation that if we don't feel safe, our brains won't turn off. To complicate matters, many with post-traumatic stress also struggle with looming nightmares before bed. What approaches might we take for such a scenario?

This is less about specific tools one might use and more to put words to that struggle. If we've done all the other stuff for a good night's rest—temperature, schedule, light exposure and so on—and we're still having trouble, it could be that we just don't feel safe in our own homes. Could installing a security system in the house improve sleep quality? Maybe we need a weighted blanket to signal the nervous system that there is a comforter nearby. Or possibly, we need to put words to the potential discomfort of the nightmares. By naming something, our relationship to it changes.

Name what the dream is composed of. Perhaps set an intention before bed that you want to pay attention. Prolonged exposure therapy is based on the idea that the more you attend to the thing you fear, the better able you become at extinguishing that fear response. Over time, could it be that by fully describing what is in the dream and setting intentions to pay attention to it while you sleep, that that process could produce a deeper understanding of your story, of what might still be left unresolved?

> # A dream that is not understood remains a mere occurrence; understood it becomes a living experience.
> *—Carl Jung*

The dream world is a space we cannot easily place under scientific scrutiny. Thus prescriptive techniques for handling upsetting dreams are more anecdotally based than anything. Some psychoanalysts are trained to conduct dream analysis and can indeed illuminate underlying memories that are screaming to be heard, but can only speak while the body is asleep. Other dreams seem more like noise than anything. Some theories of dreams are that they are the mind's attempt at practicing future scenarios and contending with them in the hypothetical unconscious space. Still others suppose that dreams are nothing but static, excitations of a complex mind. Yet the latter theory hardly seems plausible in light of how so many dreams have a structure to them and are not merely random blips of memory.

Whatever the case, we don't fully understand exactly what is going on in the mind while dreaming, nor what the full purpose of dreaming is. What we can surmise, though, is that if we don't feel safe in the place where we rest our heads, that fear has a high potential of showing up in how we dream.

I was camping one summer just north of Mammoth Lakes, CA, off a dirt road a mile from the highway. There were a few other dispersed campers in the area, but I had my site all to myself. The temperature was nice and cool, I'd just finished watching my fire turn to little embers, I'd had a challenging day of exercise, and was well away from artificial light. I should have been set up for a great night's rest. But when I laid down, my brain immediately played a little movie scene where an ax murder found my tent. I kept disputing the thoughts and reassured myself that I would be perfectly fine. I'd slept soundly in the woods many times before, but something about that night, I couldn't get that image out of my head. At one in the morning I woke up with a start after having dreamt of that exact movie scene. Maybe if I'd had my usual bear spray laid next to my head, that would have been enough to end that mental chatter and allow me to sleep.

One last note on shaking off bad dreams: if you find yourself waking up from a disturbing dream, get your body moving as soon as possible. There's something about activating the muscles that can windshield-wipe away the residue of the dream space. Conversely, to remember dreams better, do the opposite, that is, lay still while intentionally recalling the dreams for a better chance at remembering them later.

FASTING

The practice of fasting (the act of quitting food or some other source of sustenance for a longer period of time than usual) has been used as a physical and spiritual healing practice for about as long as physical and spiritual healing practices have been around. While there are many things someone could give up for a prolonged duration and gain some type of mental and physical benefit, we will mostly focus on fasting from food as that is the type of fast most of us could benefit from the most[11] (with social media and news likely being close seconds).

Fasting can extend life span, help the body burn fat, decrease inflammation, allow a high degree of internal detoxification to

---

11   For those who struggle more with not consuming enough nutrients, a media fast may be a much better approach with this practice. Becoming more disciplined about eating a whole food-based breakfast may be what is needed rather than the discipline to skip.

occur, enhance our ability to draw energy from both fat and carbs, and helps the practitioner to become more aware of how hunger sensations come and go. Fasting is also a powerful neuro-protective stimuli for TBI. In hunter-gatherer days, it was quite common to go long stretches without food, and the body needed to be able to access energy to hunt effectively even if it had been a while since the last feeding.

We still have those mechanisms today, but they are rarely, if ever, tapped into.

In a world where we have an abundance of available calories, our sensation to eat is more often based off habit and time of day than real hunger. Just like rhythms with sleep cycles, we also have hormonal rhythms cuing us to eat. Ghrelin is the main driver of hunger and it, like other hormonal signals, will come and go simply with the passing of time. But the cue to eat doesn't mean we have to follow that cue. Feeling hungry is not a bad thing, contrary to so many Snickers commercials. We can ignore that sensation and it will pass, gaining a greater degree of freedom over our physical sensations. This is the practice of "urge surfing," recognizing an urge, choosing not to indulge, and allowing it to pass.

Every living human has an enormous storehouse of usable energy in their bodies at all times in the form of stored fat. Even the leanest among us can survive in excess of a month without food. When we continue to eat the type of food that signals the body to *store*, rather than to metabolize, usable energy, the body will adapt to relying on consumed food instead of stored food energy, which is housed in the dense fat tissue everyone possesses.

Consider for a moment how it could possibly make biological sense for an obese person to feel hungry all the time. Why should someone with tens of thousands of calories in storage not be able to use that energy on a moment's notice? There exists this dependence on quickly burned energy from the modern diet which prevents the body from accessing what is generally a "cleaner" burning fuel source. Cleaner in the sense that metabolizing a greater proportion of our fuel from fat tends to produce lower levels of inflammation in the long run.

At a very basic level, the Western diet has many foods which combine carbs and fats in high amounts; cakes, cookies, pancakes with butter, foods with grains and oil, that sort of thing. This ratio of macronutrients doesn't exist in nature. Either you eat whole fruits or honey with healthy carbs, or your eat meat which has only fat and protein. But never one food with carbs and fat (coconuts being an exception, but even pure coconut manna does have nearly the same hormonal response when consumed as Standard American Diet foods). The problem with this combo is that you have a nutrient which promotes hunger (carbs) paired with a satiety nutrient, promoting fullness due to the higher density of calories (fat). When we eat both together, the signal from carbs wins. It's not a good messaging combo: stay hungry despite a high calorie load. This is to say nothing of the problem with synthesized fats and sweeteners.

Two chapters ago, I introduced the idea that 70% of what's in the grocery stores cannot be considered a "species appropriate diet." One of the reasons for this is the fact that—apart from the carb/fat combo—the body has a much more difficult time discerning the nutrient content of fake foods. For example, when refined sugar and artificial sugar are combined in a single product, like in many energy drinks, your body gets a stimulation of sweetness that it translates as something calorie rich—which gives the brain happy signals, because in the wild, this means you've found some honey or berries which fuel your ability to sprint away quickly from dangers or toward your next big meal. However, when all that artificial stuff hits the gut, it turns out that many of the sweet signals were false signals and the "real" sugar arrived in a foreign form devoid of all the information necessary for a smooth translation into the gut and ultimately as a usable energy source.

Imagine you had a gas gauge in your car that changed its indicator about every third day, but it was irregular. Some days it displayed too high a number and other days too low. Some days it is correct, but you, as the driver, never know which days are the correct days.

What do you think such a gauge would do to your frequency of gas station fill ups? Would you err on the side of putting in more fuel more often?

Likewise, the body, when fed false food information in the form of fake fats and fake sugars, will send a greater number of signals in the body to fill up as often as possible because it has learned that the satiety signals of foods aren't as reliable as once thought.

For most of us, the drive to eat food can overwhelm other sensations. And skipping a meal, (horrors!) is not a practice endorsed by the American food culture at large. However, doing so with regularity has a profound impact on our self-control, cellular health, and so many other things. To return to a more health-promoting hormone signaling pattern, fasting is the ultimate reset tool.

Part of a meditation practice is becoming familiar with sensations but not being ruled by them. In the words of Pastor Dallas Willard, "Feelings are good servants, but they are disastrous masters." Fasting is the practice of placing feelings in a subordinate role to our executive minds. It allows us to feel the feeling of hunger (a hunger for food, information, or anything else to quench boredom) and work through the peaks and valleys with a measured response instead of with an unconscious reaction to snack.

While in one sense, fasting is giving up a physical desire and cutting ourselves off from immediate satisfaction, it has the potential to ultimately give us a greater sense of fulfillment when we introduce the contrast of lack to constant satisfaction. Humans need to live in a Goldilox zone of *optimal deprivation* (avoiding the extremes of skin and bones or terminal obesity), and some type of fasting allows us to do this. When we voluntarily create this contrast of deprivation, we may indeed find that when it does come time to consume, whether that be food, media or other indulgence, we enjoy the experience all the more. The experience becomes far more vivid when we make a decision to say no to the body and yes to the higher self.

What to Expect When Fasting

To begin, if fasting from food is something that hasn't been done much, download the app called Zero (or set some other timer) and see how long it takes for you to become hungry after eating dinner. See how 12 hours feels, then 16, then consider working your way up to 24. While we start to see significant increases in growth hormone after about 16 hours calorie-free, as we get started, the main point is to control cravings, to exert top-down control on hunger sensations. So, if that just means going a full eight hours from dinner to breakfast where before it was only six, then that is a start. The number of hours is relevant to the physiological changes, but the primary aim of fasting, as we're discussing here, is more as a spiritual practice, one of killing the ego. Insofar as pausing your food intake accomplishes this, you're on the path of returning power to your higher mind.

Fasting will likely be more difficult if one's diet is very high in quickly burned carbohydrates; going a full 24 hours out the gate will be tough. Fat cells tend to store toxins and when we fast, and the body isn't primed to tap into those, they are metabolized and released. The body has a robust filtering mechanism that helps shuttle those toxins away, but when released at a higher volume, it may result in a sort of hungover detox feeling. You can offset this somewhat by drinking some kind of calorie-free salt source. Carbohydrate-heavy foods hold water and electrolytes in the body, so by abstaining, some compensation with salts may be necessary. The same holds true if one were to pursue a low-carb diet.

With practice, the body will become more adept at using fat as a fuel source. It does this by turning on portions of your genetic code that are otherwise dormant on the Standard American Diet. It turns out that carbs are *not* the body's preferred fuel source,[12] but ketones, a by-product of fat, are. Ketones are only produced at a high volume when carbs are significantly reduced in the diet or if you're fasting.

Ketones are a fuel that both the heart and brain can run off of as well as an extremely powerful anti-inflammatory signaling molecule—they may be the reason fasting can have positive effects in the case of brain injury. But they will only get switched on in a significant amount during longer fasts (16+ hours) or if the diet is sufficiently low in breads, crackers, cakes, sugars of all varieties, and other carb-heavy foods.

One last consideration. I realize that acute cravings for things can feel impossible to surf through. We might appraise that craving as our source of truth for what our next behavior needs to be. If you are dealing with constant cravings for packaged foods, the automatic response is to eat to make those cravings go away. The behavior ostensibly is there to satisfy what we believe we truly

---

12 The rationale for carbs being the body's fuel source reminds me of the myth the Army used to proport about how most of the body's heat is lost through the head. This conclusion came after evaluating someone's core temperature while they were standing bundled in the cold…without wearing a hat. The body prefers carbs if you train it to via a constant consumption thereof.

need.[13] But are the craving killers truly satisfying the desire? Like a hydra that regrows two heads out of one that's been chopped off, the cravings keep coming back and often we need more and more of what, at first, appeared to be the thing that was going to satisfy. If it's truly satisfying, why do we need so much more to fill that desire?

Food…for thought.

PLAY

Taking time out for low stakes fun should be considered another necessity, not just in support of an otherwise busy life, but in a psychological recovery process. Why do we play and what exactly is a game?

Playing is an engagement in some sort of unstructured or semi-structured activity with very low stakes. There may or may not be an objective. If there is only an object with no objective, then you're probably playing with a toy. When there is an objective involved and you're playing alone, then that's a puzzle. If you're playing with others, the play involves conflict. If the conflict is in accordance with rules which prevent the players from interacting, then it's a competition, like a foot race. However, if the players can interact, that's a game.

Bernard Suits, professor of philosophy at the University of Waterloo, states that "a game is the voluntary attempt to overcome unnecessary obstacles." By this definition, much of our life experience might be considered a kind of game. The difference between a game that can last 90 years or more and one lasting only a few

---

13 Breaking this cycle is often much harder than we first think. AA acknowledges that with alcohol, only a power outside of ourselves could hope to help us break the pattern. There's no beating around the bush about how powerful physical urges can be. Do you find this the case with food and media, too?

minutes to an hour or two is that in the latter case, the rules are much more clear, feedback is typically immediate, it's very clear who is on your team and who is not, and the rewards for good playing are realized right away. It's very clear who the winners and losers are. A game is a microcosm of life.

It is games that give us something to do when there is nothing to do. We thus call them "pastimes" and regard them as trifling fillers of the interstices of our lives. But they are much more important than that. They are clues to the future. And their serious cultivation now is perhaps our only salvation.
—Bernard Suits

Playing games, by the definition above, lets us practice a type of healthy conflict which in a sense mimics the grand game of life, but in a highly compressed span of time. It's important to take time out to play games because in the dynamic, complex life game, the rules are messy, we rarely get immediate feedback, it's not always clear who is on your side, and the rewards for doing well are much slower in coming, if they indeed come at all.

Games also give us permission to try, fail, improve, and repeat in a structured way. When I moved to a new part of town, to try and get to know more people in the area, I found a volleyball club that met twice a week. It had probably been ten years since I'd played and though I considered myself athletic, I was more the chase sport than the ball sport type of athlete. In any case, I found myself holding a volleyball when it was my turn to serve. Somehow,

I had positioned myself on the court so that I would start the very first match with the very first serve. With 11 pairs of eyes of people I had just met looking at me, I had to serve, a task that takes a lot more finesse than one might think. Tossing the ball up and cranking back my hand, I was milliseconds away from a collision between too much confidence and too little competence. The ball went straight into the net and the other team got the point.

But while I had some embarrassment for a moment, it took all of three seconds for everyone to forget about that serve, move on with the game, and two hours later, part ways to return to the rest of their lives. I was the only one thinking about that serve. Far more than the serve, though, I left the courts that night thinking about how much fun I'd had. It had truly been years since I felt like I was just having fun in that way, a brand of fun that bike riding, swimming, running, and lifting (or playing video games alone) doesn't reproduce. Volleyball was a venue for fun failure, a place where I can get over my false self image while enjoying the process.

Fun failure with actionable feedback done in a team setting creates a dynamic where you can almost see yourself level up while contributing to a bigger whole. It's much harder to see that process when stretched over a long time frame, so being able to see it in the context of games can provide a great relief. Too much ego in a game makes one the type of player no one else wants to play with.

Military training is all an elaborate game. One way to look at the nostalgia retired service members have when reflecting back on those long days is that they miss having people to play with. How much different is a training scenario from "the voluntary attempt to overcome unnecessary obstacles?" It's an endeavor which permits imperfect efforts with clear feedback, which builds mastery and agency, which reinforces positive boundaries and individual contribution, which provides an invitation to put intense concentration on an interesting problem, and which provides an optimal tension between competence and confidence—just the right amount of challenge to facilitate a flow state.

The types of games which fall into this kind of time out could really be any sort of ball sport played in a group or even video games. The catch with games played on a screen is that to gain the full benefit of engaging in overcoming voluntary obstacles is that it's best done with someone else who is also in the room. Still, games which incorporate some type of physical movement are going to be the best bang for your buck as it blends team play with friends and strangers, zone two cardio, and may have the added bonus of stimulating some needed vitamin D production when done outdoors.

Practicing playing games with others and cooperating in compliance with an agreed upon ruleset reminds the psyche that this is how human life is meant to be lived, a reminder with much more tangibleness than the long march of the life game.

Dance

When I was a sophomore in high school, like many boys my age, I had a crush on this girl but next to zero confidence to go and talk to her. The best I could do was to try and steal glances from her in hopes that somehow locking eyes at the right time would communicate to me that she liked me back. It was all very confusing. But one day, I worked up the courage to ask her to a dance. I waited for just the right time when I passed her in the hallway when we were both alone. I had rehearsed exactly what I was going to say. I'd put on plenty of antiperspirant. I was ready for this.

The day came. With a stomach full of butterflies, I made the approach and asked the question. Her response? "Oh, that's a shocker." She stepped back awkwardly and I did my best to change the subject, but there was to be no such ejection lever. I was gutted.

That experience, paired with the challenges of living with a nomadic family making it difficult to find stable friend groups, left an imprint on me that my fear of the opposite sex was valid. While through college, I wasn't completely useless at approaching ladies, there was still a veneer of anxiety that always went along with it. I dreaded any sort of function that involved asking a girl to dance; apart from that one barn dance at summer camp years ago, I'd had no experience. It was another decade that it occurred to me to actually take the plunge and sign up for a dance class.

I wasn't really sure what to expect, and my brain came up with about 37 different stories about reasons why I shouldn't go, but I found that about two minutes in, I saw that everyone else who was there (this was a beginner's group) had much the same kind of apprehension. That eased my mind tremendously and when I was able to get out of my head and see that everyone else here was awkward and new to this, I found myself in quite pleasant company and I found as well that the techniques came quickly to me.

Being able to see myself work toward mastery with immediate feedback from my dance partners got me hooked. I could feel my body leveling up in an activity. In the words of Brett Eldredge, I finally found somethin' I'm good at.

Happiness is the emotion the body produces when one can perceive meaningful movement toward a goal, especially when that goal is in alignment with our values. For me, mastery is one of my core values and this venue enabled this value to live, both on the social and athletic front. This tangible skill building then generalized to other areas of life, helping my overall confidence immensely.

During my ROTC days, we were visited by several high ranking officers that came now and again to conduct mentor sessions. I remember one telling me how when he was at West Point, he was taught how to box. Boxing, in his view, employed every component of combat principles: objective, offensive, mass, economy of force, maneuver, unity of command, security, surprise, and simplicity. The idea is that by learning a martial art which serves as a sort of war game, the skills then generalize to the actual war fighting.

Dance is boxing's social equivalent. It teaches you to play with boundaries, to work well with others, to be mindful of how your actions affect those around you, and that you can make mistakes and still bond with someone close to you. It builds a huge amount of confidence because the confidence starts to be backed with competence. Your self-belief that you can do the thing becomes backed up with undeniable proof of you actually doing the thing. This is the positive feedback loop that can pull us from overwhelming anxiety and depression and remind us that there are still venues where we can practice agency, fairplay, and gives us something to look forward to, that things can actually change, grow, and adapt.

It was only after my personal revelation with dance classes that I looked at the research to see if interventions had been done with those going through a trauma recovery. Sure enough, dancing interventions are well-known to serve a role on that front, even in veterans groups.

Here's one other way of looking at dancing (and group play) as it relates to mental distress. What action does the body take if someone is depressed? If there was a security camera watching that person, what movements would be captured? You might be picturing someone whose bodily movements are sort of apathetic, unenergized, hunched or tight shoulders (what are yours doing now?), downcast eyes, short steps, and a body typically not taking up a lot of space. Now, what is the body doing when dancing? The exact opposite of all of those. The action of dance, and social play in general, is a physical expression of the opposite of traumatic stress and depression.

So what are you waiting for? Bust a move.

Chronic Stress/Trauma	Play/Dance
Promotes isolation	Practices connections
Worries and ruminates	Promotes states of flow in the moment
Silences new possibilities	Every session is a new possibility
Stuck in a status quo of skill	Builds mastery
Breeds dependence on medication	Releases "medication" from within
Encourages immediate comfort	Practices controlled discomfort
Stuck in individual thoughts of dread	Shares experiences of awe
Promotes depression	Promotes expression
External Locus of Control (Things happen to me)	Internal Locus of Control (I happen to things)
The world is unfair, it will never change, and the future is hopeless.	People can play fair, I can meaningfully contribute, and I can get better in the future.
Focuses on perpetual life-threats	Practices accepting the rules of life and builds competence at handling defeat
Creates barriers to relationships according to rigid rules	Practices relationships with semi-flexible rules
Fears human touch	Practices human touch with healthy social boundaries
Anxiety → Withdraw → Relief → Regret → More Anxiety	Anxiety → Participation → Mastery → Fun → Anxiety Relief
Encourages Self-Deprecation	Builds Self-Confidence in all areas of life
Hides from new challenges	Accepts new challenges
Generates a sense of detachment	Generates a sense of belonged around a shared activity
Severs the individual from culture	Builds culture itself
Promotes brain rigidity	Promotes brain plasticity
Failure is associated with death	Failure is associated with improvement
Stress response	Challenge response

CHAPTER 11

THE TEST OF THE BOX

W E'VE LOOKED AT HOW finding wisdom through the recovery of moral injury often has to do with holding tension between seemingly opposite things. A Chinese proverb says that all truths are found in paradoxes. If we are in a season of recovery, it might be helpful to know what that space feels like. When there is tension between opposites, it might produce within us a feeling of discombobulation. But what else should we feel during a season like this?

There will be days which contain a melange of doubt, hope, despair, and laughter—days which feel like someone took every bottle of assorted food coloring and put one drip of each into a bowl of water. And our heart can have a hard time making sense of it all. The encouragement here is this: this is what healing feels like.

These awkward tensions between the polars of, say, the joys of being in the company of small children and the horrors of intrusive memories of war, mean that you're still in the fight. This is the felt sensation of participating in the human drama. While at times it might feel like the pull of gravity has been reversed, maybe multiple times in a single day, this is what healing feels like.

With that in mind, I have good news and bad news.

The bad news: we are all going to suffer in the future.

The good news: we get to choose whether that suffering serves us or kills us.

More good news: if we choose to allow suffering to do its work, then even the bad news becomes good news.

We must all suffer from one of two pains: the pain of discipline or the pain of regret. The difference is discipline weighs ounces while regret weighs tons.
—Sean Covey

In the 2021 film, *Dune*, the main protagonist, Paul Atreides, must go through a trial before he is permitted to speak about and pursue his dreams. This is the test of the box. At the behest of his mother—who in her own way was fulfilling the mother's hero's journey by allowing her son to experience the trials of the world after having raised him—Paul must follow instructions from the Reverend Mother, whose role is to sort the wheat from the chaff.

"The test is simple. Remove your hand from the box and you die."

"What's in the box?" Paul asks.

"Pain," was the only response.

During the test, flashes of burning sand come and go from Paul's mind. The Reverend Mother says to him, "An animal caught in a trap will gnaw off its own leg to escape. What will you do?"

More flashes of fire, burning palm trees, broken and burnt bodies. Paul's mother, outside the room, utters a kind of litany.

I must not fear.
Fear is the mind-killer.
Fear is the little-death that brings total obliteration.
I will face my fear.
I will permit it to pass over me and through me.
And when it has gone past I will turn the inner eye to see its path.
Where the fear has gone there will be nothing. Only I will remain.

Until at last, Paul is shown overcoming the pain, now looking the Reverend Mother directly in the eyes. The crescendo sounds.

"Enough!" she says. "You've proven you can rule yourself. Now you must learn to rule others, something none of your ancestors learnt."

Paul succeeds in a small-scale hero's journey of initiation wherein he allows himself to pass through a purifying fire, burning off his old way of being. Only then, he is able to conquer worlds, experience love, and understand the meaning of his dreams.

This is the ordeal of moral injury recovery.

Hard choices, easy life.
Easy choices, hard life.
—*Stoic Proverb*

It will take time, but tiny steps will compound.

> No discipline seems pleasant at the time,
> but painful. Later on, however, it produces a
> harvest of righteousness and peace for those
> who have been trained by it.
> —*Hebrews 12:11, NIV*

In aviation, there is the 1 in 60 rule which states that for every degree a plane is off its trajectory, it will be 1 mile off its destination for every 60 miles flown. So, if a plane takes off at the equator to travel the world but is off by 1 degree, it will be nearly 500 miles off its destination.

This is how making small changes compounds; it's a one-degree difference made each day. Then those changes become habits. Then those habits become your new way of life that mark your character and destiny. And the thing is, there's no staying the same; we all either make gradual improvements or experience gradual decline. It's not possible to remain static.

It's also not reasonable to turn everything around in a very short time. Often, when someone sees a glimmer of hope, a new way of doing things that could lead to huge change, poor expectations are made early. The big, sexy life transformations are expected up front, and when those do not come about so quickly, it's easy to give up. But as the saying goes, the journey of a thousand miles begins with a single step…and is only ever composed of single steps. A 0.1% improvement everyday is a 36.5% improvement every year. What if you kept that up for 10 or 20 years? What would you be like then?

Every day presents its own little hero's journey, and you can count on each day rendering a different result, because life change is not linear. It will always have ups and downs. Pursuing the horizon always involves rolling water. Relapses are a very common part of the process itself. It doesn't mean failure; it means you've learned something else about yourself and what you can do to grow and experience new life after moral injury. If you do experience a relapse, it is only proof that you're making an effort to grow. The backslide actually demonstrates that there was a place that you reached to even backslide *from*. Backslides aren't possible without some sort of forward progress to begin with. We strive for progress, not perfection.

This daily journey presents a choice: to make suffering work for us, or to be victimized by it. Do we work out when we don't want to? Do we go through the pain of accepting and sharing our story? Do we hold ourselves accountable while kicking sugar dependence? Do we voluntarily engage in the hard labor of changing our home environment to make it work for healing? Do we choose to forgive or to resent?

Life after moral injury is realizing that if something is hard, if something feels challenging, if there emerges an ego desire to quit even though we know it's the right thing to do, these are all indicators that you're on the right path.

What will you do?

Return in 200 Words:

- ☐ Accept that you will never be the same person again.
- ☐ Forgive yourself and others daily.
- ☐ Read stories of tragedy and triumph.
- ☐ Write, speak, and share your story.
- ☐ Create art when speech fails.
- ☐ Set intentions for each day and evaluate how well you met those intentions at the end of the day.
- ☐ Workout at the threshold of your ability. Train with heavy objects. Run, ride, swim, row, sprint. Three days a week minimum. Get at least 5500 steps daily.
- ☐ Meditate and pray every day.
- ☐ Breathe through your nose.
- ☐ Give thanks verbally and in writing, often.
- ☐ Routinize bedtime and wake time. Make the bedroom dark, cool, and clean.
- ☐ Eat organic foods you can pick directly from the ground or purchase at a butcher shop. Take omega-3, magnesium, and vitamin D supplements. Consume organ meats, bone broth, and "adaptogenic" herbs. Ruthlessly remove all vegetable, soybean, and canola oils, refined sugar, and modern wheat from the diet.
- ☐ When possible, get enough sunlight to sustain a tan.
- ☐ Remove plastic food containers and hormone-disrupting products from your life.
- ☐ Prioritize time out with food or media fasting.
- ☐ Play games and dance with others.
- ☐ Cultivate experiences of awe by routinely encountering the natural world away from modern distractions.

REFERENCES

INTRODUCTION

Erickson, M. (2020, March 11). Alcoholics Anonymous most effective path to alcohol abstinence. *Stanford Medicine News Center*, https://med.stanford.edu/news/all-news/2020/03/alcoholics-anonymous-most-effective-path-to-alcohol-abstinence.html

CHAPTER 1

Rosenhan, D. L. (1974). On Being Sane in Insane Places. *Perspectives in Abnormal Behavior*, 509–524. https://doi.org/10.1016/b978-0-08-017738-0.50055-7

Crocq, M. A., & Crocq, L. (2000). From shell shock and war neurosis to posttraumatic stress disorder: a history of psychotraumatology. *Dialogues in Clinical Neuroscience, 2*(1), 47–55. https://doi.org/10.31887/DCNS.2000.2.1/macrocq

Percy, J. (2014). *Demon Camp: A Soldier's Exorcism.* Scribner.

Shay, J. (1995). *Achilles in Vietnam.* Simon & Schuster.

Galatzer-Levy, I. R., & Bryant, R. A. (2013). 636,120 Ways to Have Posttraumatic Stress Disorder. *Perspectives on Psychological Science, 8*(6), 651–662. https://doi.org/10.1177/1745691613504115

Jung, C. G., & Carrington, H. R. F. (1967). Commentary on "The Secret of the Golden Flower." Routledge and K. Paul.

Kolb, H., Kempf, K., Röhling, M. et al. Insulin: too much of a good thing is bad. *BMC Med* **18**, 224 (2020). https://doi.org/10.1186/s12916-020-01688-6

Raven, M., & Parry, P. (2012). Psychotropic Marketing Practices and Problems. *The Journal of Nervous and Mental Disease, 200*(6), 512–516. https://doi.org/10.1097/nmd.0b013e318257c6c7

Admin. (2021, April 23). Mental health drug prescriptions on the rise. Insurance Journal. https://www.insurancejournal.com/news/national/2021/04/22/610924.htm

Rak, C. F., & Ingersoll, R. E. (2016). Psychopharmacology for Mental Health Professionals: An integrative approach. Brooks/Cole.

Moncrieff, J., Cooper, R. E., Stockmann, T., Amendola, S., Hengartner, M. P., & Horowitz, M. A. (2022). The serotonin theory of depression: A Systematic Umbrella Review of the evidence. Molecular Psychiatry. https://doi.org/10.1038/s41380-022-01661-0

Gregory, A. (2022, July 20). Little evidence that chemical imbalance causes depression, UCL scientists find. The Guardian. https://www.theguardian.com/society/2022/jul/20/scientists-question-widespread-use-of-antidepressants-after-survey-on-serotonin

Culpepper, L., Davidson, J. R., Dietrich, A. J., Goodman, W. K., Kroenke, K., & Schwenk, T. L. (2004). Suicidality as a Possible Side Effect of Antidepressant Treatment. Primary care companion to the Journal of clinical psychiatry, 6(2), 79–86. https://doi.org/10.4088/pcc.v06n0206

Jung, C. G. (1932). Psychology and religion. Yale University Press.

Eliot, T. S. (2019). Four quartets. Faber & Faber.

CHAPTER 2

Walker, S. F. (2002). *Jung and the Jungians on myth: An introduction*. Routledge.

Shay, J. (2003). Achilles in Vietnam: Combat trauma and the undoing of character. Scribner.

Johansen, T. K. (2022). Productive knowledge in ancient philosophy: The concept of technê. Cambridge University Press.

Pirsig, R., & Pressman, L. (1999). *Zen and the Art of Motorcycle Maintenance*. Landmark Audiobooks.

Levers, L. L. (2012). Trauma counseling theories and interventions. Springer Pub.

Guan, F., Xiang, Y., Chen, O., Wang, W., & Chen, J. (2018). Neural Basis of Dispositional Awe. Frontiers in behavioral neuroscience, 12, 209. https://doi.org/10.3389/fnbeh.2018.00209

Schurtz, D. R., Blincoe, S., Smith, R. H., Powell, C. A., Combs, D. J., & Kim, S. H. (2011). Exploring the social aspects of goose bumps and their role in awe and envy. *Motivation and Emotion, 36*(2), 205–217. https://doi.org/10.1007/s11031-011-9243-8

Herbert, F. (1984). *Dune*. Putnam.

Profane: Search online etymology dictionary. Etymology. (n.d.). Retrieved August 18, 2022, from https://www.etymonline.com/search?q=profane

Eliade, M, & Trask, W. R. (1987). *The sacred and the profane: The nature of religion*. Harcourt Brace Jovanovich.

Haidt, J. (2015). *The happiness hypothesis: Putting ancient wisdom to the test of modern science*. Cornerstone Digital.

Bernhardt, P. C., Dabbs Jr, J. M., Fielden, J. A., & Lutter, C. D. (1998). Testosterone changes during vicarious experiences of winning and losing among fans at sporting events. *Physiology & Behavior, 65*(1), 59–62. https://doi.org/10.1016/s0031-9384(98)00147-4

CHAPTER 3

Dispenza, J. (2018). Breaking the habit of being yourself: How to lose your mind and create a new one. Hay House.

Leaf, C., (2015). *Switch on your brain: The key to peak happiness, thinking, and health*. BakerBooks, a division of Baker Publishing Group.

Lipton, B. H. (2011). *The Biology of Belief*. Hay House UK Ltd.

Peterson, J. B., & Fogra, J. (2022). *Beyond order: 12 more rules for life*. Penguin Books.

Schwartz, R. C. (2013). Moving from acceptance toward transformation with Internal Family Systems therapy (IFS). Journal of Clinical Psychology, 69(8), 805–816. https://doi.org/10.1002/jclp.22016

A., V. der K. B. (2015). *The body keeps the score: brain, mind, and body in the healing of trauma*. Penguin Books.

Wolynn, M. (2022). *It didn't start with you: How inherited family trauma shapes who we are and how to end the cycle*. Vermilion.

CHAPTER 4

Riedel S. (2005). Edward Jenner and the history of smallpox and vaccination. *Proceedings (Baylor University. Medical Center)*, 18(1), 21–25. https://doi.org/10.1080/08998280.2005.11928028

Taleb, N. N. (2013). *Antifragile*. Penguin.

Paris, J. (2023). *Myths of trauma: Why adversity does not necessarily make us sick*. Oxford university press.

Trauma: Search online etymology dictionary. Etymology. https://www.etymonline.com/search?q=trauma

Watson, J. P., Gaind, R., & Marks, I. M. (1971). Prolonged exposure: A rapid treatment for phobias. *BMJ*, *1*(5739), 13–15. https://doi.org/10.1136/bmj.1.5739.13

American Psychological Association. (n.d.). *Stress in America™ 2020: A National Mental Health Crisis*. American Psychological Association. Retrieved November 15, 2021, from https://www.apa.org/news/press/releases/stress/2020/report-october.

Snyder, C. R. (2021). *The Oxford Handbook of Positive Psychology*. Oxford University Press.

Enthusiasm: Search online etymology dictionary. Etymology. (n.d.). Retrieved February 28, 2022, from https://www.etymonline.com/search?q=enthusiasm

CHAPTER 5

Three Initiates (1908). *The Kybalion: A Study of the Hermetic Philosophy of Ancient Egypt and Greece*. Chicago: The Yogi Publication Society.

Lewis, C. S., (2017). *The C.S. Lewis signature classics*. HarperOne, an imprint of HarperCollinsPublishers.

CHAPTER 6

Consume (v.). Etymology. (n.d.). Retrieved March 2, 2022, from https://www.etymonline.com/word/consume#:~:text=consume%20(v.),to%20consume%22%20(12c.)

Jung, C. G., & Jacobi, J. (1973). *C.G. Jung, psychological reflections: A new anthology of his writings, 1905-1961.* Princeton University Press.

Hooper, P. L., Hooper, P. L., Tytell, M., & Vígh, L. (2010). Xenohormesis: health benefits from an eon of plant stress response evolution. Cell stress & chaperones, 15(6), 761–770. https://doi.org/10.1007/s12192-010-0206-x

CHAPTER 7

Lipton, B. H. (2003). *The Biology of Belief.* Spirit 2000, Inc.

A., V. der K. B. (2015). The body keeps the score: Mind, brain, and body in the transformation of trauma. Penguin Books.

English sanskrit dictionary and translation - shabdkosh. (n.d.). Retrieved May 23, 2022, from https://www.shabdkosh.com/dictionary/english-Sanskrit

Lanza, R., Berman, B., & McKnight, A. (2009). Biocentrism: How life and consciousness are the keys to understanding the true nature of the universe. BenBella.

Dictionary.com. (n.d.). *Failure definition & meaning.* Dictionary.com. Retrieved May 23, 2022, from https://www.dictionary.com/browse/failure

Sacks, O. (1999). *Awakenings.* Random House.

Smedes, L. B. (1996). *The Art of Forgiving.* Moorings.

Solženicyn, A., & Willetts, H. T. (1978). *The gulag archipelago.* Harper & Row.

Burton, L. R. (2020). The Neuroscience and Positive Impact of Gratitude in the Workplace. Journal of Medical Practice Management, 35(4), 215–218.

Goleman, D., & Davidson, R. J. (2018). *Altered traits: Science reveals how Meditation Changes Your Mind, brain, and body.* Avery, an imprint of Penguin Random House LLC.

Centers for Disease Control and Prevention. (2022, May 3). *Disparities in suicide.* Centers for Disease Control and Prevention. Retrieved May 23, 2022, from https://www.cdc.gov/suicide/facts/disparities-in-suicide.html

Tedeschi, R.G., & Calhoun, L.G. (1996). *The Posttraumatic Growth Inventory: Measuring the positive legacy of trauma.* Journal of Traumatic Stress, 9, 455-471.

Flow, the secret to happiness. (2004). Mihaly Csikszentmihalyi: Flow, the secret to happiness | TED Talk. Retrieved August 4, 2023, from https://www.ted.com/talks/mihaly_csikszentmihalyi_flow_the_secret_to_happiness.

CHAPTER 8

Dyer, K. F., & Corrigan, J.-P. (2021). Psychological treatments for complex PTSD: A commentary on the clinical and empirical impasse dividing unimodal and phase-oriented therapy positions. Psychological Trauma: Theory, Research, Practice, and Policy, 13(8), 869–876. https://doi.org/10.1037/tra0001080

Schnyder, U., Bryant, R. A., Ehlers, A., Foa, E. B., Hasan, A., Mwiti, G., Kristensen, C. H., Neuner, F., Oe, M., & Yule, W. (2016). Culture-sensitive psychotraumatology. European journal of psychotraumatology, 7, 31179. https://doi.org/10.3402/ejpt.v7.31179

Attia, P. (2023). *Outlive.* Penguin Random House USA.

Michopoulos, V., Vester, A., & Neigh, G. (2016). Post-traumatic stress disorder: A metabolic disorder in disguise? Experimental Neurology, 284, 220–229.

Schuch, F. B., Vancampfort, D., Richards, J., Rosenbaum, S., Ward, P. B., & Stubbs, B. (2016). Exercise as a treatment for depression: A meta-analysis adjusting for publication bias. *Journal of Psychiatric Research, 77*, 42–51.

https://doi.org/10.1016/j.expneurol.2016.05.038

Sumner, J. A., Nishimi, K. M., Koenen, K. C., Roberts, A. L., & Kubzansky, L. D. (2020). Posttraumatic stress disorder and inflammation: Untangling issues of bidirectionality. Biological Psychiatry, 87(10), 885–897. https://doi.org/10.1016/j.biopsych.2019.11.005

Berk, M., Williams, L. J., Jacka, F. N., O'Neil, A., Pasco, J. A., Moylan, S., Allen, N. B., Stuart, A. L., Hayley, A. C., Byrne, M. L., & Maes, M. (2013). So depression is an inflammatory disease, but where does the inflammation come from? BMC Medicine, 11(1). https://doi.org/10.1186/1741-7015-11-200

Araújo, J., Cai, J., & Stevens, J. (2019). Prevalence of optimal metabolic health in American Adults: National Health and Nutrition Examination survey 2009–2016. Metabolic Syndrome and Related Disorders, 17(1), 46–52. https://doi.org/10.1089/met.2018.0105

Muralidharan, S., & Mandrekar, P. (2013). Cellular stress response and innate immune signaling: Integrating pathways in host defense and inflammation. *Journal of Leukocyte Biology, 94*(6), 1167–1184. https://doi.org/10.1189/jlb.0313153

Alam, Q., Zubair Alam, M., Mushtaq, G., A. Damanhouri, G., Rasool, M., Amjad Kamal, M., & Haque, A. (2016). Inflammatory process in Alzheimer's and Parkinson's diseases: Central role of cytokines. *Current Pharmaceutical Design, 22*(5), 541–548. https://doi.org/10.2174/1381612 822666151125000300

Donath, M. Y., & Shoelson, S. E. (2011). Type 2 diabetes as an inflammatory disease. *Nature Reviews Immunology, 11*(2), 98–107. https://doi.org/10.1038/nri2925

Wolf, R., & Cordain, L. (2017). *The Paleo Solution: The original human diet.* Victory Belt Publishing.

Davis, W. (2019). Wheat belly: Lose the wheat, lose the weight, and find your path back to health. Rodale Books.

Shanahan, C., & Shanahan, L. (2018). *Deep nutrition: Why your genes need traditional food.* Flatiron Books.

Firth, J., Gangwisch, J. E., Borisini, A., Wootton, R. E., & Mayer, E. A. (2020). Food and mood: how do diet and nutrition affect mental wellbeing?. *BMJ (Clinical research ed.), 369*, m2382. https://doi.org/10.1136/bmj.m2382

Wang, C.-H., Wang, C.-C., & Wei, Y.-H. (2010). Mitochondrial dysfunction in insulin insensitivity: Implication of mitochondrial role in type 2 diabetes. Annals of the New York Academy of Sciences, 1201(1), 157–165. https://doi.org/10.1111/j.1749-6632.2010.05625.x

Mercola, J. (2021). *Emf*D: 5G, Wi-Fi & cell phones - hidden harms and how to protect yourself.* Hay House.

U.S. Department of Health and Human Services. (n.d.). Endocrine disruptors. National Institute of Environmental Health Sciences. Retrieved November 29, 2021, from https://www.niehs.nih.gov/health/topics/agents/endocrine/index.cfm

CHAPTER 9

HandWiki Liu. (2022, October 24). *Dukkha*. Encyclopedia. https://encyclopedia.pub/entry/30933#:~:text=Dukkha%20 (%2F%CB%88du%CB%90k%C9%99%2F%3B%20 P%C4%81li,and%20painfulness%20of%20mundane%20life.

Sapolsky, R. M. (2004). *Why zebras don't get ulcers: The acclaimed guide to stress, stress-related diseases, and coping.* Henry Holt and Co.

Gold, P. W., Drevets, W. C., Charney, D. S., & Drevets, W. C. (2002). *New insights into the role of cortisol and the glucocorticoid receptor in severe depression.* Biological Psychiatry, 52(5), 381–385. https://doi.org/10.1016/s0006-3223(02)01480-4

Nolen-Hoeksema, S. (2020). *Abnormal Psychology.* McGrawHill Education.

Ballenger, J. C., Davidson, J. R. T., Lecrubier, Y., Nutt, D. J., Marshall, R. D., Nemeroff, C. B., Shalev, A. Y., & Yehuda, R. (2004). Consensus statement update on posttraumatic stress disorder from the International Consensus Group on Depression and Anxiety. *Journal of Clinical Psychiatry,* 65(Suppl. 1), 55-62.

Ludwig, V. M., Bayley, A., Cook, D. G., Stahl, D., Treasure, J. L., Asthworth, M., Greenough, A., Winkley, K., Bornstein, S. R., & Ismail, K. (2018). Association between depressive symptoms and objectively measured daily step count in individuals at high risk of cardiovascular disease in South London, UK: a cross-sectional study. *BMJ open, 8*(4), e020942. https://doi.org/10.1136/bmjopen-2017-020942

McGonigal, K. (2021). *The joy of movement: How exercise helps us find happiness, hope, connection, and courage.* Avery, an imprint of Penguin Random House LLC.

Moncrieff, J., Cooper, R. E., Stockmann, T., Amendola, S., Hengartner, M. P., & Horowitz, M. A. (2022). The serotonin theory of depression: A Systematic Umbrella Review of the evidence. *Molecular Psychiatry.* https://doi.org/10.1038/s41380-022-01661-0

Raison, C. L., & Miller, A. H. (2012). The evolutionary significance of depression in Pathogen Host Defense (Pathos-D). *Molecular Psychiatry, 18*(1), 15–37. https://doi.org/10.1038/mp.2012.2

Araújo, J., Cai, J., & Stevens, J. (2019). Prevalence of optimal metabolic health in American Adults: National Health and Nutrition Examination survey 2009–2016. Metabolic Syndrome and Related Disorders, 17(1), 46–52. https://doi.org/10.1089/met.2018.0105

Schuch, F. B., Vancampfort, D., Richards, J., Rosenbaum, S., Ward, P. B., & Stubbs, B. (2016). Exercise as a treatment for depression: A meta-analysis adjusting for publication bias. *Journal of Psychiatric Research, 77,* 42–51. https://doi.org/10.1016/j.jpsychires.2016.02.023

Fetzner, M. G., & Asmundson, G. J. G. (2014). Aerobic exercise reduces symptoms of posttraumatic stress disorder: A randomized controlled trial. *Cognitive Behaviour Therapy, 44*(4), 301–313. https://doi.org/10.1080/16 506073.2014.916745

Whitworth, J. W., Nosrat, S., SantaBarbara, N. J., & Ciccolo, J. T. (2019). Feasibility of resistance exercise for posttraumatic stress and anxiety symptoms: A randomized controlled pilot study. *Journal of Traumatic Stress, 32*(6), 977–984. https://doi.org/10.1002/jts.22464

Saint Louis University. (2019, August 21). Meaningful PTSD symptom decrease may lower type 2 diabetes risk. ScienceDaily. Retrieved November 16, 2021 from www.sciencedaily.com/releases/2019/08/190821142734. htm

Klimek, C., Ashbeck, C., Brook, A. J., & Durall, C. (2018). Are injuries more common with CrossFit training than other forms of exercise? *Journal of Sport Rehabilitation, 27*(3), 295–299. https://doi.org/10.1123/ jsr.2016-0040

Sisson, M., & Kearns, B. (2016). *Primal endurance.* Primal Blueprint Publishing.

Owen, N., Healy, G. N., Matthews, C. E., & Dunstan, D. W. (2010). Too much sitting: the population health science of sedentary behavior. *Exercise and sport sciences reviews, 38*(3), 105–113. https://doi.org/10.1097/ JES.0b013e3181e373a2

Ma, X., Yue, Z.-Q., Gong, Z.-Q., Zhang, H., Duan, N.-Y., Shi, Y.-T., Wei, G.-X., & Li, Y.-F. (2017). The effect of diaphragmatic breathing on attention, negative affect and stress in healthy adults. *Frontiers in Psychology, 8.* https://doi.org/10.3389/fpsyg.2017.00874

Diaphragm - definition, meaning & synonyms. Vocabulary.com. (n.d.). https:// www.vocabulary.com/dictionary/diaphragm#:~:text=The%20Greek%20 word%20di%C3%A1phragma%20referred,contraceptive%20first%20 surfaced%20in%201933

Encyclopædia Britannica, inc. (n.d.). *Muscle and lung receptors.* Encyclopædia Britannica. Retrieved November 17, 2021, from https://www.britannica. com/science/human-respiratory-system/Muscle-and-lung-receptors.

Weston A Price Foundation. (2018, July 19). *Weston A. Price, DDS.* The Weston A. Price Foundation. https://www.westonaprice.org/health-topics/ nutrition-greats/weston-a-price-dds/#gsc.tab=0

Ribeiro, G. C., Dos Santos, I. D., Santos, A. C., Paranhos, L. R., & César, C. P. (2016). Influence of the breathing pattern on the learning process: a systematic review of literature. *Brazilian journal of otorhinolaryngology, 82*(4), 466–478. https://doi.org/10.1016/j.bjorl.2015.08.026

McKeown, P. (2016). *The oxygen advantage: Simple, scientifically proven breathing techniques to help you become healthier, slimmer, faster, and Fitter.* William Morrow, an imprint of HarperCollinsPublishers.

YouTube. (2023). *Mewing: How to Be More Attractive, Breathe Better and Live Longer | Dr. Mike Mew EP 180. YouTube.* Retrieved August 8, 2023, from https://www.youtube.com/ watch?v=aMK3EGn26HU&ab_channel=MikhailaPeterson.

Carney, S. (2019). What doesn't kill us: How freezing water, extreme altitude, and environmental conditioning will renew our lost evolutionary strength. Scribe Publications.

Swan, S. H., & Colino, S. (2021). *Count down: How our modern world is threatening sperm counts, altering male and female reproductive development, and imperiling the future of the human race.* Scribner, an imprint of Simon & Schuster, Inc.

Carlsen, E., Giwercman, A., Keiding, N., & Skakkebaek, N. E. (1992). Evidence for decreasing quality of semen during past 50 years. BMJ (Clinical research ed.), 305(6854), 609–613. https://doi.org/10.1136/ bmj.305.6854.609

Gillespie, C. F., Almli, L. M., Smith, A. K., Bradley, B., Kerley, K., Crain, D. F., Mercer, K. B., Weiss, T., Phifer, J., Tang, Y., Cubells, J. F., Binder, E. B., Conneely, K. N., & Ressler, K. J. (2013). Sex dependent influence of a functional polymorphism in steroid 5-α-reductase type 2 (SRD5A2) on post-traumatic stress symptoms. *American Journal of Medical Genetics Part B: Neuropsychiatric Genetics, 162*(3), 283–292. https://doi.org/10.1002/ ajmg.b.32147

Reijnen, A., Geuze, E., & Vermetten, E. (2015). The effect of deployment to a combat zone on testosterone levels and the association with the development of posttraumatic stress symptoms: A longitudinal prospective Dutch military cohort study. *Psychoneuroendocrinology, 51,* 525–533. https://doi.org/10.1016/j.psyneuen.2014.07.017

Costas-Ferreira, C., Durán, R., & Faro, L. R. F. (2022). Toxic Effects of Glyphosate on the Nervous System: A Systematic Review. *International journal of molecular sciences, 23*(9), 4605. https://doi.org/10.3390/ijms23094605

CHAPTER 10

U.S. Department of Health and Human Services. (2022, March 24). *What are sleep deprivation and deficiency?*. National Heart Lung and Blood Institute. https://www.nhlbi.nih.gov/health/sleep-deprivation#:~:text=According%20to%20the%20Centers%20for,at%20least%20once%20a%20month.

National Institutes of Health (NIH). (2019, March 5). How disrupted sleep may lead to heart disease., Retrieved November 30, 2020, from https://www.nih.gov/news-events/nih-research-matters/how-disrupted-sleep-may-lead-heart-disease

YouTube. (2021). *Dr. Matthew Walker: The Science & Practice of Perfecting Your Sleep | Huberman Lab Podcast #31. YouTube.* Retrieved August 10, 2023, from https://www.youtube.com/watch?v=gbQFSMayJxk.

Walker, M. P. (2018). *Why we sleep: Unlocking the power of sleep and dreams.* Scribner, an imprint of Simon & Schuster, Inc.

Gordon, A. M., & Chen, S. (2014). The Role of Sleep in Interpersonal Conflict: Do Sleepless Nights Mean Worse Fights? Social Psychological and Personality Science, 5(2), 168–175. https://doi.org/10.1177/1948550613488952

Tedeschi, R.G., & Calhoun, L.G. (1996). *The Posttraumatic Growth Inventory: Measuring the positive legacy of trauma.* Journal of Traumatic Stress, 9, 455-471.

Randall, D. K. (2013). *Dreamland: Adventures in the strange science of sleep.* W.W. Norton & Company.

Clocks (1951), *Encyclopædia Britannica* 5, 835.

Anton, S. D., Moehl, K., Donahoo, W. T., Marosi, K., Lee, S. A., Mainous, A. G., Leeuwenburgh, C., & Mattson, M. P. (2017). Flipping the metabolic switch: Understanding and applying the health benefits of fasting. *Obesity, 26*(2), 254–268. https://doi.org/10.1002/oby.22065

Davis, L. M., Pauly, J. R., Readnower, R. D., Rho, J. M., & Sullivan, P. G. (2008). Fasting is neuroprotective following traumatic brain injury. *Journal of Neuroscience Research, 86*(8), 1812–1822. https://doi.org/10.1002/jnr.21628

Sisson, M. (2016). *Primal endurance*. Primal.

Schatzker, M. (2022). *End of craving: Recovering the lost wisdom of eating well.* Avid Reader Press.

Dallas Willard (2014). *Renovation of the Heart: Putting On the Character of Christ*, p.98, Tyndale House

Sisson, M. (2019). *The primal blueprint*. Primal Blueprint Publishing.

Sisson, M. (2020). *Keto reset diet: Reboot your metabolism in 21 days and burn fat forever.* Harmony Crown.

Suits, B. H., Newfeld, F., & Rueter, W. (1978). *The grasshopper games, life and utopia.* University of Toronto Press.

Steinberg-Oren, S. L., Krasnova, M., Krasnov, I. S., Baker, M. R., & Ames, D. (2016). Let's Dance: A Holistic Approach to Treating Veterans With Posttraumatic Stress Disorder. Federal practitioner : for the health care professionals of the VA, DoD, and PHS, 33(7), 44–49.

www.ingramcontent.com/pod-product-compliance
Lightning Source LLC
Chambersburg PA
CBHW051138120626
46547CB00012B/858